HELP!

I'M BORED!

OVER 300 CHILDREN'S ACTIVITIES
- FOR AGES 2 TO 12 -

By Janine Lynn

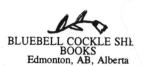

BLUEBELL COCKLE SHE
BOOKS
Edmonton, AB, Alberta

Help! I'm Bored!

Bluebell Cockle Shell Books
Edmonton, Alberta

Revised edition 1997

Canadian Cataloguing in Publication Data

Goodkey, Janine Lynn, 1963-
        Help! I'm Bored! : over 300 activities for ages 2-
12!

Revised edition.
Originally publ. under title: Mom, I'm bored!
Includes bibliographical references and index.
ISBN 0-9680809-0-1

        1. Games--Juvenile literature. 2. Creative
activities and seat work--Juvenile literature. 3.
Cookery--Juvenile literature. I. Title. II. Title: Mom,
I'm bored!

GV182.9.G66 1996   j790.1'922   C96-900723-X

Printed in Canada
Editor: Candace Weisner
Cover Artist: Laurel Hawkswell
Page 58 Origami Artist: Darlene Diver
Computer Graphics: Broderbund Software

TABLE OF CONTENTS

INTRODUCTION

Welcome to "Help! I'm Bored!" This book is a collection of successful children's activities which I've tested and tried as a youngster, as an elementary school teacher, and as a mother. I began working on this book simply because I wanted all of my favorite ideas collaborated into one book, ready to use for any occasion.

The intention of this book is to provide entertainment, while developing creativity, co-ordination, and co-operation at the same time. However, I've also included a "Learn to Read" section, found in "Fun for Little 'Uns" chapter, and numerous pages on fun ways to improve reading, writing, spelling, and math skills, found in "Partner Challenge Games" and "Rainy Day Fun".

Many of the ideas in this book are self-directed, requiring little adult assistance, and most of the activities utilize materials found in most homes/schools.

I hope you enjoy "Help! I'm Bored!", and I hope it serves you well on any occasion!

SPECIAL FUN for

LITTLE 'UNS

Ideas for Pre-Schoolers

WATER PLAY

In an outdoor wading pool (with supervision), the bath tub, or even a large basin or sink, use some of the utensils listed to have a wild, wet time!!

WATER WARES

- food coloring
- bubble bath
- a whisk
  (to stir up suds)
- funnels
- spray bottles
- turkey baster
- plastic lemon
- colander
- plastic cups/
  containers
- big spoons
- ladles
- water wheel
- rubber toys
- straws or tubing
  (to blow bubbles
   with or breathe
   through while
   under water)

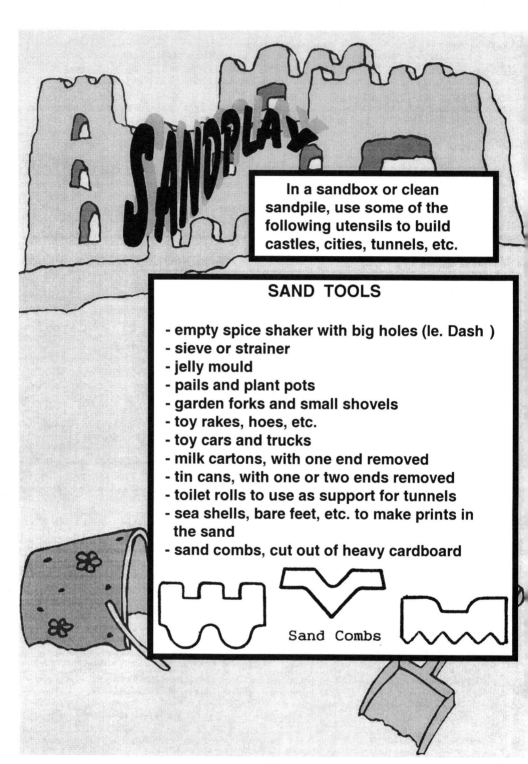

SANDPLAY

In a sandbox or clean sandpile, use some of the following utensils to build castles, cities, tunnels, etc.

SAND TOOLS

- empty spice shaker with big holes (Ie. Dash)
- sieve or strainer
- jelly mould
- pails and plant pots
- garden forks and small shovels
- toy rakes, hoes, etc.
- toy cars and trucks
- milk cartons, with one end removed
- tin cans, with one or two ends removed
- toilet rolls to use as support for tunnels
- sea shells, bare feet, etc. to make prints in the sand
- sand combs, cut out of heavy cardboard

Sand Combs

TICKLE TRUNK

Fill a box or trunk with some of the items listed. After a quick change, you can become a bride, a travel agent, a fireman, or even Superman!

- white coat (doctor, dentist, or scientist)
- dark coat and hat (policeman or mailman)
- raincoat and high boots (fireman)
- nylon netting (princess, bride, or ballerina)
- towel or cape (Superman)

- glitzy evening wear
- old-fashioned clothes
- housecoat
- wild ties
- belts/scarves
- gloves
- a variety of hats
- shoes/boots
- aprons

- artificial flowers
- wigs
- purses
- sunglasses
- jewelry
- an umbrella
- a cane
- masks
- etc.

Extras for role-playing - play money, old cheque books, travel brochures, doctor kit, toy microphone, plastic dishes, etc.

NO-FAIL PLAYDOUGH

INGREDIENTS

makes it less sticky 1/4 C.

1 C. and 2 Tbsp. flour
1/2 C. salt
1 tsp. cream of tartar (to preserve)
2 Tbsp. cooking oil
3/4 C. boiling water
Food coloring or paint/Jell-o/Kool-Aid
  powder

ANN

METHOD

Mix together first four ingredients. Add boiling water, mixed with coloring agent, and knead well. Then, use your hands and/or forks, straws, rolling pin, cookie cutters, etc. to make different shapes. (Ie. snakes, snowmen, coil basket, your name, etc.) Store in sealed container in fridge.

A4

PEANUT BUTTER PLAYDOUGH

INGREDIENTS

1 C. peanut butter
1/2 C. honey or corn syrup
1 C. icing sugar (or Graham
    Wafer crumbs, powdered
    milk, or flaked coconut)

METHOD

Mix ingredients together with clean hands.
Use a rolling pin, cookie cutters, straws, forks, garlic press (for hair or fur), or your fingers to make various creatures or shapes. Decorate with coconut, colored sprinkles, chocolate chips, raisins, nuts and seeds.

Note: With leftover dough, knead in chopped
        maraschino cherries, form balls, and roll
        in flaked coconut for a tasty treat.

A 5

CHOCO-CHUMS

INGREDIENTS
1/2 C. soft butter
3/4 C. sugar
2 eggs
2 C. flour
1/3 C. cocoa
1/2 tsp. bkg. soda

METHOD
- cream butter and sugar together.
  Add eggs and beat well. Gradually
  blend in dry ingredients.

- knead dough, and then mould into
  flat bears, fish, and other animal
  shapes (or roll out and cut with
  cookie cutters).

- decorate with colored sparkles,
  caramel chips, hard candies, etc.
  Bake at 350° F for 8 - 10 minutes.

PLASTER HANDPRINT

MAT.   - large plastic margarine or yoghurt container
        - 1 1/8 C. plaster of Paris (from lumber store)
        - 1/2 C. water
        - disposable stir stick
        - small tin pie plate
        - paper clip (Opt.)

PROC.- mIx together water and plaster of
        Paris. Stir until like thick cream.
        Pour into pie plate

      - press hand into plaster and hold it there
        for a few minutes to leave a firm impression.

      - while plaster is still soft, insert paper clip
        into top end to use as a wall hanger.

      - when plaster has hardened, remove pie
        plate, and record your name, age, and date
        on the back.

Note: - do not pour leftover plaster down the drain or toilet!! Allow it to
        dry, and then throw it away.

PAINTED TOAST

Mat. - 1/8 C. milk
- food coloring
- slice of bread
- clean pastry brush

Proc.- stir a few drops of food
coloring into milk.

- with a pastry brush,
paint a face or fancy
designs on bread.

- toast and serve.

Note - use various colors of "paint" for
more colorful designs.

FINGER PAINT

QUICK AND EASY FINGER PAINT

Mix together 1 C. water and 1/4 C. wallpaper paste. Divide mixture into portions and add food coloring or paint/Jell-o/Kool-Aid powder to color.

COOKED FINGER PAINT

In a small pot, mix together 1/2 C. flour and 1/2 C. cold water. Add 1 1/2 C. boiling water, and heat on stove until it starts to boil, stirring constantly. Cool, and add coloring as suggested above.

DIRECTIONS

Create designs on paper or water-proof surface using your fingers, fists, whole hand, or tools like forks, old combs, cake decorators, etc. When dry, use your "masterpiece" as wrapping paper, a frame for a favorite picture, or just to cut flowers, butterflies, and other designs out of. Store leftover paint in fridge.

Note: If you choose to paint on a water-proof table, T.V. tray, or other hard surface, preserve your completed work as follows: Lay a paper on design, smooth your hand over it, and carefully lift up from the corner.

FINGER PRINTING

MATERIALS

- stamp pad
- paper
- pen or felt markers

PROCEDURE

- press your finger or thumb onto stamp pad. Then, press it firmly onto paper.

- create insects, animals, people, etc. by adding eyes, ears, legs, tail, etc. with a pen or markers.

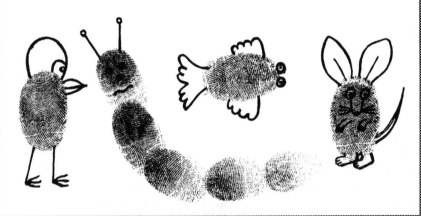

POLKA-DOT PICTURES

MATERIALS

- hole punch (Kids love to use these!)
- colored paper or magazines
- glue

PROCEDURE

- punch out a little pile of holes from colored paper or magazines.

- glue them onto a piece of paper to create a picture.

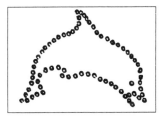
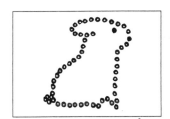
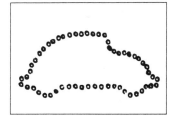

BINGO BLOTS

MATERIALS

- *bingo blotters of different colors*
- *paper*
- *pen or felt markers*
- *newspaper, to protect table (Bingo blotters stain!)*

PROCEDURE

- *cover working area with newspaper.*
- *on paper, use bingo blotters to create people animals, insects, etc.*
- *use a pen or felt marker to add eyes, mouth, legs, etc.*

TOOTHPICK ART

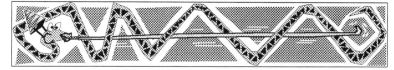

MATERIALS

- toothpicks
- felt markers
- glue
- paper

PROCEDURE

- shade toothpicks with different colored felt markers.

- glue toothpicks onto page to create a picture or design.

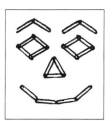
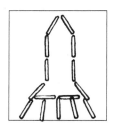

PAPER BAG MASKS

MATERIALS

- large paper bag
- crayons or felt markers
- scissors
- tin foil, tissue paper, yarn, etc. (opt.)

PROCEDURE

- place bag over your head. Ask someone older to mark locations for eye and arm holes.
- remove bag from head and cut holes.
- draw or glue on eye lids, nose, mouth, ears, etc.
- wear your mask to perform plays, but be careful not to trip!

BUILD-A-BAND

KAZOO - fold a 7.5 cm (3") circle of waxed paper over one end of a toilet roll. Secure with a rubber band. Poke a small pencil hole about 2.5 cm (1") from that same end. Resting your mouth on one side of open end of tube, hum "doo-doo" into it to make a raspy, vibrating sound.

TAMBOURINE - toss a handful of dry rice or seeds into a tin pie plate. Cover with a second pie plate and sew the two edges together with yarn.

SANDBLOCKS - glue a piece of sandpaper onto three sides of two wooden blocks. Let dry, and rub the sandblocks together to make a swishing sound.

KITCHEN BAND IN A JIFFY

CYMBALS - clang two pot lids together.
DRUM - beat a pot or bucket with a spoon.
STICKS - rap two wooden spoon handles together.
SPOONS - tap the backs of two spoons together on your knee.

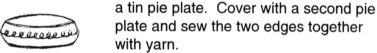

COUNTING CRUNCHIES

Part. - 2 or more players

Mat. - 1 or 2 die/dice
- bowl of Cheerios (or peanuts, grapes, raisins, etc.)

Obj. - to shake the die to earn the most "crunchies".

Proc.- wash your hands, please.

- in turn, players shake the die (or dice) and take that number of crunchies from bowl.

- when bowl is empty, after someone shakes the exact number to empty it, count your crunchies. The player with the most is the winner.

- now, feast!

NATURE BINGO

MAT. - Nature Bingo card below
- 16 small stones

PROC. - alone or with a friend, place a marker (stone) on the square of every item you find.

- you have a "Bingo" once you complete a line or a black-out.

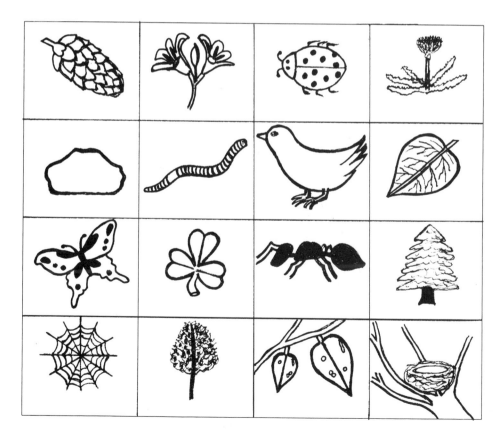

DONUT BIRD FEEDER

MAT. - 1 donut
- 2 disposable plastic lids
- 1 piece of string or yarn
  (about 50 cm or 20" long)

PROC.- sandwich donut between plastic lids.
- thread string through hole in lids
  and donut as shown. Tie a big, fat
  knot on bottom.
- with an adult's help, hang from
  house or tree for birds to enjoy.

HAIRY HARRY

MATERIALS

- 1 tin can
- permanent markers, bits of felt, or colored paper
- potting soil
- grass seed

PROCEDURE

- on one side of can, make a face for Harry using markers, felt, or colored paper.

- fill can with soil.

- sprinkle grass seed on top and keep moist.

- in a few days, Harry will have some green hair.

LEARN TO READ!!

PLEASING PATTERNS

Ask someone to read pattern (repetitive) books to you often, such as "The Gingerbread Man" and "The Hungry Caterpillar". Before long, you will be able to "read" the stories yourself, first by memory, and later, by reading the words!

BECOME AN AUTHOR

Draw pictures on a piece of paper or in an empty booklet. Recite your story or description to someone older while he/she records it, one sentence per page. "Read" story often, to a parent, sibling, or even your dolls or pets!

PHOTO FUN

Design your own mini photo album with any photos you can scrounge up. Dictate a short caption to be printed under each photo. "Read" through album often.

HOUSEHOLD LABELS

With help, print the name of many household objects onto recipe (or computer) cards, or strips of paper. (Ie. stove, fridge, dresser, mirror, etc.) Tape cards to corresponding objects, and "read" them often.

LOGICAL LABELS
   Cut out labels from common household containers.
(Ie. milk/juice cartons, cereal boxes, Jell-o boxes, etc.).
Save in a special bag or box and "read" through often.

THEME PACKS
   With help, record 5 - 10 words of the same theme
onto recipe (or computer) cards, or cardboard strips.
(Ie. colors, shapes, transportation, etc.) Add
appropriate pictures. Link together with a curtain hook.
Make more theme packs and "read" through often.

ALPHABET BOOK
   Print one letter of the alphabet in the top corner of
each page of a scribbler. Add pictures that begin with
the letter recorded. "Read" each word as you look
through the book.

BUILD - A - RHYME
   With help, copy a well-known poem or nursery rhyme
onto chart paper. Cut into sentence or word strips.
Add pictures, and practice putting rhyme back together.

STORY TAPES
   Frequently listen to story tapes and follow along in
the book. - - or, record your own story, ringing a bell
when it's time to turn the page. If you wish, mark the
play button with a green sticker and the stop button
with a red sticker.

"FUN FOR LITTLE 'UNS" LIST

INDOOR ACTIVITIES

COLORED MACARONI PICTURES
Sprinkle several drops of food coloring into a bowl of dry macaroni. Mix well, and spread out onto a cookie sheet to dry. Make macaroni of different colors, and glue onto heavy paper to create a picture. (Note: If using for "Kitchen Sandbox" below, mix well, every so often, to prevent mold.)

KITCHEN SANDBOX
Partly fill a large plastic tub with cornmeal, rice, or colored macaroni mentioned above. Then, use cups, spoons, colanders, sieves, etc. to dig, scoop, and measure "sand".

SORTING SENSE
Gather a collection of simple objects like buttons, shells, bottle caps, coins, paper clips, rubber bands, etc. Sort them into egg carton or muffin tin sections according to color, size, type, etc. Store in carton. - - or, for a change, sort a deck of cards, or help your mom by matching socks from the laundry!

MECHANO MUDDLE
Make your own Mechano Box by filling a box with old mechanical objects to tinker with. (Ie. cameras, clocks, etc.)

DANDY DOMINO TIPPING
On a hard, flat surface, stand up Dominos one behind the other to make a long winding path. Then, knock the first one into the second. What happens? For more Domino fun, ask someone to teach you how to play the game "Dominos", starting with seven each.

FELT BOARD FROLIC

Glue a piece of heavy felt (from fabric store) onto sturdy cardboard or wood panelling. Cut shapes out of different colored felt to tell stories with on felt board. - - or, cut shapes out of heavy paper and glue piece of felt or Velcro to back.

FAST-GROWING BEAN PLANTS

Soak two or three bean seeds in water overnight so they plump up. Then, press seeds into indoor soil in plant pot, about 3 cm (1") apart. Fill in holes and water gently. Place in sun, and water when dry. Beans should sprout in less than a week.

TIME FOR TAPES

Listen to a story or nursery rhyme tape while you follow along in the book. Your mom may want to mark the play button with green tape or stickers for you, and the stop button with red.

BELT IT OUT

Sing and do actions to fun songs/verses like Eency Weency Spider, Baby Bumblebee, Five Little Monkeys, Teddy Bear, We're Going to the Zoo, Forty Years on an Iceberg, Head and Shoulders, Swimming, The Grand Old Duke of York, etc.

CARPET TUNNEL

Roll up a scrap piece of carpet (or a foam mattress) to make a tunnel to crawl through. Tie to secure, if you wish.

BOX PLAYHOUSE

Cut a door, windows, etc. out of a large fridge or freezer box to make a little playhouse. Use paint, wallpaper, etc. to decorate.

MILK CARTON CONSTRUCTION
Collect a large number of rinsed out milk or juice cartons and use them to build houses, tunnels, bridges, etc. Paint, if you wish.

CRAZY CAMPING
Cover chairs and tables with large blankets and sheets to make a tent. Toss in sleeping bags, a flashlight, etc. for added fun. Alternative: With permission, set up a real tent in the basement or the back yard.

RADICAL RAMPS AND TERRIFIC TUBES
Build ramps and/or tunnels by balancing skinny boards, heavy cardboard strips or tubes, or vacuum hoses on chairs, stairs, or railings. Tie or tape to secure, if you wish, and run toy cars down ramps.

BEANBAG BANTER
Use a beanbag (easier to handle than a ball) to play catch with a friend, to balance on your head as you walk, or to toss into a bucket or at some plastic targets. You can make your own beanbags by turning in edges and sewing around a 16 x 32 cm (6.5 x 13 ") piece of heavy fabric folded in half and partly filled with beans.

TALENTED TOES
Hold a crayon or felt pen (or chalk) between your toes and try to draw pictures on paper taped to the floor (or chalkboard).

STENCIL SCRIBBLES
Make impressive pictures and improve your co-ordination by drawing around commercial (or home-made) tracers, stencils, or cookie cutters.

"FUN FOR LITTLE 'UNS" LIST continued . . .

FRUIT LOOP NECKLACE

String Fruit Loops or Cheerios onto shoestring licorice to make an edible necklace. . . . or thread beads, pieces of straws, or colored macaroni (mentioned earlier in this list) onto a colorful shoelace.

PUDDING PAINT

Make your favorite flavor of pudding according to the directions. Then, use clean kitchen utensils or fingers to paint designs on sturdy paper, a cookie sheet, or a water-proof table. Have a few licks now and then.

MARSHMALLOW SNOWMAN

Make " 'Mallow Men" using large marshmallows, raisins, chopped up maraschino cherries, etc. held together with toothpicks.

MAGNIFICENT MURALS

Using paint and paintbrush, or large felt markers, make a colorful mural on chart paper or a large paper bag opened up.

LOOPY LACING

Glue a simple picture onto cardboard or styrofoam. Cut out through both layers. Use a hole punch to make holes every 1" around picture. Tie a knot in one end of a long colorful shoelace, and lace in and out of holes.

OUTDOOR ACTIVITIES

PSYCHEDELIC SNOWMAN
Pour 1 C. water and 1 tsp. paint powder (or 20 drops food coloring) into a spray bottle. Then, decorate a snowman, or draw pictures on a fresh bed of snow, with colored spray.

SUPER SNOW SHAPES
Lie on a fresh bed of snow to make snow angels, butterflies, rocket prints, etc.

SHARP SHADOWS
With a friend on a sunny day, use chalk to trace each other's shadow as you strike a funny pose. Can you fit into each other's shadow?

WONDERFUL WET-PRINTS
Pour water into a cake or bread pan. Dip your bare feet or hands into water and make wet-prints on the sidewalk.

SPLASHY SIDEWALK PAINTING
Use one of your dad's large paintbrushes (or a plant mister) to create pictures on the sidewalk, using water mixed with a little paint powder, food coloring, or Kool-Aid powder.

BUG BINOCS
Make your own set of binoculars by glueing or taping two toilet rolls together. Paint and decorate. Take them on your next "Bug Hunt" to help you find interesting creatures.

GLORIOUS GAMES
With friends, play fun games like "Red Light, Green Light", "What Time is it Mr. Wolf?", " I Wrote a Letter to My Love", etc.

Creative

ARTS &

CRAFTS

CREATIVE PAINTING

HERE ARE SOME ALTERNATIVE MATERIALS TO USE TO MAKE PAINTING MORE EXCITING!!

PAINT - paint tablets, or 2 Tbsp. tempera paint powder (from craft/teacher's store or stationer) added to a mixture of 6 Tbsp. water and 1Tbsp. wallpaper paste. This makes paint thick while conserving paint powder.

PAINTING TOOLS

- old toothbrushes
- old comb
- sponges
- Q - tips
- cotton balls
- end of a rope
- old pot scrubber
- corn cob
- feather
- pine cone
- pine needle branch
- sticks
- paint roller
- hands/feet
- straw (to blow paint)

PAINTING SURFACES

- newspaper (classifieds)
- paper bags
- wrapping paper
- wallpaper
- cardboard
- boxes or cartons
- tin or paper plates
- tin foil
- boiled eggs
- heavy fabric
- windows
- wood
- sandpaper
- rocks
- sidewalks

BREAD DOUGH ART

INGREDIENTS
3/4 C. and 2 Tbsp. hot water
1/2 C. salt
2 C. white flour
2 tsp. glycerine (opt.)
Egg white or mayonnaise
Paint, varnish, or nail polish (opt.)

METHOD
- in a bowl, stir together hot water and salt for one minute. Add flour, and knead well until soft and smooth. (Add more flour or water if necessary.)

- form shapes with your hands, or roll out dough to 1/4" thickness and press with cookie cutters. To make hair or straw, squeeze through a garlic press. To hang an ornament, press a paper clip halfway into top of shape, or poke a small hole into top.

- place on cookie sheet and bake at 325°F (or 300°F for thin projects) for 1/2 to 3 hours, depending on thickness of project. To prevent cracking, dampen lightly or glaze with mayonnaise or egg white a few times during baking.

- dough is done when hard all over, even at the thickest part. (Check by poking with a skewer.)

- when cool, paint or varnish to preserve.

Note: To add color to dough, add food coloring, paint powder, or cocoa to hot water.

PAPER MACHÉ

PASTE — mix together 1/2 C. wallpaper paste and 2 C. warm water (or 1 C. flour and 1 1/8 C. cold water). If thickens too much, add a few drops of water.

METHOD — dip newspaper strips about 3 cm (1") wide into paste. Use two fingers to press off excess and smooth onto project.

PAPER MACHÉ MARACA

Smooth many layers of strips onto burnt out light bulb to make about 2 cm (3/4") thickness on all sides. Set aside to completely dry for a few days. Then, smash maraca against a hard surface to break bulb inside, so as to make a rattling sound when you shake it. Paint to decorate.

PAPER MACHÉ MASK

Draw outline of eyes and mouth on one side of a round balloon. Smooth five or six layers of strips onto balloon, but be sure not to cover eye or mouth holes, or back half of balloon. Set aside to dry for about two days. Then, pop balloon with a pin. Trim around edge of mask, and around eye and mouth holes with scissors. Paint to decorate. Let dry. Tie string through small holes made on each side of mask to hold onto face.

SANDCAST FOOTPRINT

Mat. - 1 C. water
- 2 1/4 C. plaster of Paris (from lumber store)
- large yoghurt or margarine container
- disposable spoon or stick
- sandbox or beach

Proc.- dampen a small area of sand. Pack down and
smoothen it.
- make a footprint in sand, about 2 cm (1/2") deep.
- mix together water and plaster of Paris to thickness
of a milkshake. Pour mixture to fill in footprint.
- leave to completely dry for an hour or more.
- carefully lift up footprint and brush off loose sand.
- record date and your name on back.

Other Sandcasting Ideas
- handprint
- sea shell or bone fossils
- nameplates (print letters backwards
and in reverse order in sand)

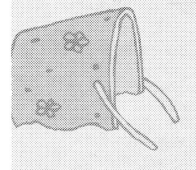

 # PAPER BAG PUPPETS

Mat. - paper lunch bags
- colored paper
- crayons and scissors
- pipe cleaners, cotton balls, etc. (opt.)

Proc.- on colored paper, draw and cut out puppet face. Glue
onto flap (bottom) of lunch bag.

- glue on tongue to stick out from under flap (opt.)

- with crayons or colored paper, add eyes, ears, etc.

- put your hand inside bag and flap mouth.

Variation - Cut slit in open end of bag and fold down puppy
ears, as shown. Draw or glue on face. Stuff
with newspaper and staple down ears.

B5

PAPER PLATE PUPPETS

Mat. - paper plate
- felt markers
- scissors
- yarn, bottle caps, tin foil, etc. (opt.)
- tape and ruler

Proc.- draw and decorate your puppet's face with
materials suggested.
- tape ruler onto back.

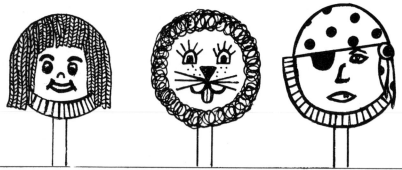

PUPPET THEATRE
Perform puppet plays from behind a table set on its
side, or a large box with the top, bottom, and one side
cut out, as well as a rectangular opening in the front.

PAPER PENDANT

Mat. - piece of cardboard
- construction paper of several colors
- pencil
- scissors and white glue
- sandpaper
- a magnet, chain, or leather tie
- clear nail polish or white glue and water (opt.)

Proc.- draw a simple shape onto cardboard,
about 6 cm (2.5") wide. Cut out.

- use cardboard shape to trace thirty more shapes
onto construction paper, exactly the same size.
Cut out.

- glue all the shapes together, making sure you
spread glue over the whole surface of each
shape. Let dry overnight.

- over a period of days or weeks, sand
around the edges at an angle. If you
want more colors to show through, sand
some spots on the top surface as well.

- coat pendant with clear polish, or one
part glue mixed with one part water.

- glue magnet on back to hang it on fridge, or ask
an adult to drill a hole through it and hang it from
a chain or leather tie.

PAPER BEADS

Mat. - small piece of cardboard
- old magazines or wallpaper scraps
- scissors and glue
- thin knitting needle
  (or pen refill or round toothpick)
- yarn or light string
- shellac (or clear nail polish, or white glue
  mixed with a little water) (Opt.)

Proc.- make a cardboard tracer to look like this:

4 cm

30 cm

- trace twenty or so triangles onto magazine
  pages or wallpaper. Cut out.

- roll each triangle around knitting needle (or
  alternates) starting at the wide end of paper.
  Dab a little glue on tip to prevent unravelling.

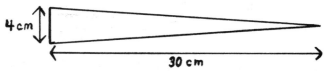

- make more beads, and then string them.

- brush beads with shellac or alternates (Opt.)

PRESSED FLOWERS

Mat. - thin, freshly-picked flowers
and/or greenery
(Ie. pansies, wild roses, etc.)
- old telephone book
- 4 or 5 heavy books

Proc.- flatten flowers, face-up
or on their side, between
pages in a telephone book.
Pile heavy books on top.

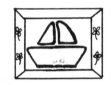

- leave for a month or so
until all the moisture has
been completely absorbed.

- use to make pretty bookmarks
(using wide ribbon and clear
Mac-Tac), or to decorate photo
album pages, picture frames,
writing paper, etc.

WHEAT WOVEN HEART

Mat.- wheat sheaves (from craft store, or cut in early August when bottom 10-15 cm (4-6") is still green. Hang bundles to dry for a few weeks. When dried, break above bottom "knee" and slide leaf sheaf away.)
- scissors and thin string
- ribbon and/or dried flowers
- wallpaper tray

Proc.- soak sheaves in warm water in wallpaper tray for 1/2 hour, or 2 hours for black-bearded wheat.

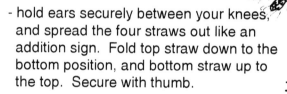

- tie four long, well-matched straws just below the ears.

- hold ears securely between your knees, and spread the four straws out like an addition sign. Fold top straw down to the bottom position, and bottom straw up to the top. Secure with thumb.

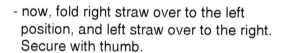

- now, fold right straw over to the left position, and left straw over to the right. Secure with thumb.

- repeat steps over and over until you have a plait about 15 cm (6") long. Secure with string, and then make a second identical plait. Tie these two plaits together where the plaiting ends.

- bend the two plaits down to form a heart shape and tie at the bottom. (The unplaited straw will become a post in the centre.) Cut excess straw ends off about 2 - 3 cm (1") below tie.

- decorate heart with ribbon and/or dried flowers.

Note- search a library or craft store for more wheat weaving ideas.

BRAIDED MAT

Mat. - 3 long, thin strips of colorful cloth
- 1 piece of string
- thread and needle

Proc. - tie ends of strips of cloth together with a big knot.

- with string, tie this end to a table leg or chair.

- tightly braid strips together. Sew ends to secure.

- remove from table leg and roll into a coil. Sew to secure, and use as a coaster, hot pot mat, Barbie Doll floor mat, etc.

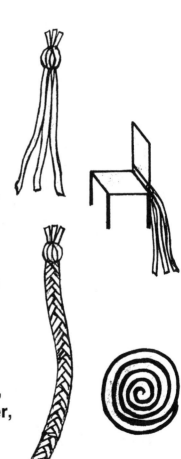

EMBROIDERY FUN

    With a pencil, draw a simple picture or design onto a piece of burlap or fabric. Secure tightly in an embroidery hoop. Using a blunt needle and yarn or embroidery thread, follow the diagrams below to complete the picture.

Running Stitch

Backstitch

Cross Stitch

Satin Stitch

Chain Stitch

Blanket Stitch

MATERIALS - 1 or more balls of yarn
- 2 knitting needles

CASTING ON

1. With end of yarn, make a slip knot.

Slip loop onto left-hand needle, and tug end of yarn to tighten.

2. Put tip of right-hand needle through loop.

3. From the back, wind working yarn around needle.

4. Bring yarn through loop and put this new loop onto left-hand needle.

5. Repeat steps 2 - 4 until you have 20 loops on needle, or as many as you need.

P L A I N   K N I T T I N G

1. Put point of right-hand needle
   through back of first loop on
   left-hand needle.

2. Wind yarn back and around
   point of right-hand needle.

3. With point of right-hand needle,
   pull yarn through first loop.

4. Slip the stitch off left-hand
   needle.

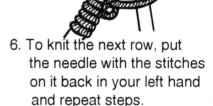

5. Repeat steps until all of the
   stitches are worked onto
   right-hand needle. Keep
   pushing the stitches toward
   tip of needle so they're easy
   to work with.

6. To knit the next row, put
   the needle with the stitches
   on it back in your left hand
   and repeat steps.

B I N D I N G   O F F - when project is to desired length.

1. Knit first two stitches in usual
   way.

2. Put point of left-hand needle
   down through stitch knitted
   first.

3. Lift this stitch over the one
   above it and over point of
   needle.

4. Repeat steps with every
   stitch. When only one stitch
   is left, cut a tail of about
   15 cm (6") and pull it through
   this last stitch. Slide stitch off
   needle and pull tight.

SPOOL KNITTING

Mat. - 1 large wooden thread spool
     (or small roll of tape)
  - hammer
  - 4 - 6 small finishing nails
  - ball of yarn

Proc.- hammer nails every 1 cm or so (about 1/2")
    around hole, evenly-spaced.

- drop one end of yarn
  through hole. Wind
  yarn around each nail
  until back at starting nail.

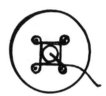

- hold yarn against the first nail, above the
  loop. Using a crochet hook or thin nail, lift
  loop over the working yarn and nail.

- repeat procedure on next nail, and so on, but
  keep yarn quite loose. Tug at tail fairly often.

- when cord is to desired length, cut yarn and
  thread end through each loop as you lift it off
  the nail. Pull tightly and tie a knot.

- use as a belt or hair tie, or wind into a coil and
  sew to make a hot pot mat or doll house rug.

Note: To make a toque, tank top, tube pillow, or
    toy snake, hammer nails every 2 cm (3/4")
    around a 20 or 25 cm (8-10") wooden
    embroidery hoop.

CROCHETED CREATIONS

MAT. - crochet hook and ball/s of yarn

SLIP KNOT
Make as shown, about 10-12 cm (4-5") from yarn end.

CHAIN STITCH
Reach hook through loop and pull working yarn through. Now, pull yarn through new loop, again and again, until chain is to desired length, with last loop still on hook.

SINGLE CROCHET STITCH
Reach hook through top two threads of second link and pull working yarn through. Then, pull yarn through two loops now on hook. Repeat step in following links to the end of the row. Then, make one extra stitch to keep your work even. Count your stitches, every so often, to be sure you still have the number you started with.

BINDING OFF (when project is to desired length)
At the end of the last row, make one more chain stitch. Cut tail and pull through loop, pulling tight. Then, make a knot and cut tail off.

SIMPLE CROCHETED PROJECTS

SQUARE PROJECTS

Hot Pad - start with about 30 - stitch chain.
Make a square and bind off.

Pillow - start with chain length sized to fit
Cover   pillow. Make two squares and
          slipstitch together around pillow.

RECTANGULAR PROJECTS

Finger Puppet - start with 16 - stitch chain.
Crochet 8 - 10 rows, to fit

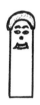 around finger. Slipstitch long
edges and one end together.
Use yarn, fabric, etc. to make
puppet face.

Scarf - start with 30 - 35 stitch chain. Crochet
to desired length and bind off.

Toque - start with 36 - 40 stitch chain. Crochet
rows needed to fit width of head.
Slipstitch two short ends together and
bind off, leaving a 40 cm (16") long tail.
Thread darning needle with tail and
weave in and out of second row down
from top edge, all around project. Pull
tightly and tie securely.

CIRCULAR PROJECTS

Coasters, Hot Pad,
Doily, or Pillow Cover - start with 6 or 7 stitch chain. Slip hook through first link of chain and work two stitches into it. Repeat step all around circle until you get back to your first stitch. On the next round, alternate working one stitch and two stitches into every link. On the third round, work two stitches into every link, and so on.

Note: Check out a craft store or library for more stitch types (Ie. double, ribbed, etc.) or more project ideas.

CRAYON FABRIC PAINTING

With parent supervision, melt crayon scraps in an empty tuna or soup can over boiling water. Working quickly, paint unique pictures or designs on an old t-shirt or apron. To make colors permanent, cover designs with a fabric scrap and press with a hot iron.

HOME-MADE PAINT TABLETS

In separate styrofoam egg carton sections, mix different colors of paint powder with a little water. Leave to harden.

EGGS-CITING EGG CREATURES

Using a tack, make a hole in each end of an egg. Blow through one hole to empty contents into a dish. Immerse egg shell into water mixed with food coloring or Kool-Aid powder. When dark enough, dry off egg and use felt markers or bits of fabric and paper to add features. Glue on Cheerios for feet.

NEON SIDEWALK CHALK

Mix together 3 T. plaster of Paris, 2 T. paint powder (bright color), and 1/4 C. water. Pour into two solid-stick deodorant lids greased with butter. Let dry for a half hour. Then, loosen sides and knock chalk out.

PRECIOUS PET ROCK (or Paperweight)

Glue well-shaped rocks together to make the body of a person or animal. Add features with felt markers, bits of felt or fabric, pipe cleaners, etc.

MAGNIFICENT MIRROR IMAGE

Glue one half of a congruent picture (same on both sides) onto paper. Then, draw and color blank side to complete the picture.

String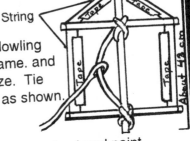

CLEVER KITES

Make your own kite using light dowling (or straws joined together) as the frame. and large plastic garbage bags cut to size. Tie frame together and tape on plastic, as shown.

SCENIC SAND PAINTINGS

Mix small amounts of sand with different colored paint powder, mixed with a few drops of water to bring color out, or cocoa, dry mustard, paprika, etc. Then, draw a simple picture on heavy paper, spread glue inside one outline, and sprinkle colored sand onto it. Lightly shake off excess, and then fill another outline with a different color.

SPIFFY SAND JAR

Layer different colored sand (described above) in a fancy jar. Glue on lid and use as a paperweight.

PERFECT PRESERVATION

Break apart the stems of ferns or leafy greens by cutting several small slices in or hammering ends. Place stems in a mixture of one part glycerine and three parts hot water for 1 - 2 weeks, until soft and dried. Add to dried flower arrangements.

SMART STRING DESIGNS

Mark points every 2 - 3 cm (1") around the edge of a piece of wood. Pound in a finishing nail at each point. Tie one end of yarn to corner nail, and wrap it around other nails to make interesting designs.

CREATIVE CRAFTS

Check out a library or craft store to learn how to do fun crafts like PAPER TWILLING, MACRAME, GIMPING, etc.

BUBBLE MANIA

Mat. - 4 C. warm water
- 1/2 C. good quality dish soap (Ie. Dawn)
- a little food coloring or paint/Kool-Aid powder (opt.)
- 3 - 4 Tbsp glycerine, from drugstore, or corn syrup
  (Opt., but makes larger, more durable bubbles.)

Proc.- pour ingredients into ice cream pail or cake pan.

- stir well, but not so that mixture froths up.

- using any of the Bubble Makers listed below, dip
  one end of tool into mixture to get film across the
  end. Then, lightly blow through it from the side,
  or wave it in the air to form bubbles. Twist off, if
  necessary.

- Store leftover bubble mixture in bottle or jar.

BUBBLE MAKERS

- plastic straw
- a cluster of straws taped together
- tin can with ends removed
- plastic bottle with end removed
- plastic holder for 6-pack
- plastic strawberry basket
- funnels
- whisks
- slotted spoons
- spaghetti measuring spoon
- small cookie cutters
- paper towel roll (tape bottom
  edge to make water-proof)

C1

PAPER WATER BOMB

Mat. - square piece of paper, at least 20 x 20 cm (8 x 8")
(Draw designs on paper if you wish.)
- water

Proc. - fold up on the broken lines
and back on the dotted lines,
as shown. Leave paper
folded on the last broken line.

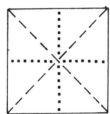

- holding onto ends of triangle,
push into centre and lay flat on
table to form a smaller triangle.

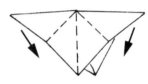

- fold outer point of top flaps up
to top point. Flip over and
repeat on other side.

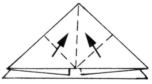

- fold outer corners of top flap to
centre. Flip and repeat.

- curl top flaps down and tuck into
pockets of little triangles, as far
as possible. Flip and repeat.

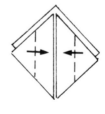

- blow into open end to inflate cube. If necessary,
poke a skewer inside hole and push out sides.
Fill with water, and cool off your friends by
landing a water bomb right beside them ! !

FROZEN STATUES

Part. - at least 3 participants

Obj. - to pose as the best "statue".

Proc.- the "sculptor" swings each player around by the arm and then lets him/her go. Each twirled player must freeze into whatever position he/she ends up in.

- once all statues are "frozen", the sculptor chooses his/her favorite statue, who then becomes the next sculptor.

Var. - Once all players are "frozen", the sculptor watches closely to eliminate any statues caught moving. The last statue still frozen becomes the next sculptor.

Mat. - scissors and string
 - colorful streamers or wide ribbon
 - brightly colored tape and/or stickers
 - clothespin and playing card (or thin cardboard)

HANDSOME HANDLEBARS

Cut four or five thicknesses of streamers (about 20 cm or 8" long) into thin strips. Secure one end with a long piece of string and tie onto handlebar. Make one for both sides.

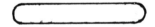

SPIFFY SPOKES

Weave streamers or ribbon in and out of the wheel spokes. Tie ends to prevent unravelling.

FLASHY FRAME

Decorate frame and/or fenders with colorful stickers, or with strips of tape to make fancy stripes.

CLATTER CARD

Clothespin the playing card to the rear fender brace, with the tip of the card between the spokes. Then, clatter away.

NATURE SCAVENGER HUNT

Part. - 1 or more participants

Mat. - pencil, and lists below
    - ice cream pail

Obj. - to find all of the nature items in one list.

Proc.- alone or racing with friend/s, explore your yard to find and check off the items in either List 1 or 2.

    - in your pail, only collect items that can be returned safely and without damage.

    - after 10 - 15 minutes, add up your score/s. Some items are worth two points, as shown.

LIST 1	LIST 2
- tree bark	- twig
- dandelion	- worm (2)
- acorn (2)	- dead grass
- dead leaf	- spider web (2)
- seed	- rock
- bone (2)	- pine needle
- flower petal	- ladybug (2)
- sand	- something white
- mushroom (2)	- clover
- insect	- larva, on a leaf

BUG CATCHER

Mat. - 2 straws, one slightly larger than the other
 - 1 small circle of nylon stocking, about
   3 cm (1") in diameter
 - tape

Proc.- fold piece of nylon over one end of
   smaller straw, and fit into one end of
   larger straw.
 - tape to secure.
 - to shorten, if you wish, cut off about 1/3
   of each straw at outside end.

Use - sneak up on a bug. Place large end of
   bug catcher over bug and suck. Plug
   this end with your finger to keep bug in.
   Then, blow it into a container or cage to
   examine more closely before freeing it
   once again.

Mat. - rubber boots
      - plastic spoon **POND STUDY**
      - clear plastic cups (or yoghurt tubs)
      - ice cube tray or styrofoam egg carton
      - magnifying glass and dip-nets
      - waterscope (See following page)
      - adult permission and/or supervision

Proc. - use your equipment to kindly capture, sort, and
        examine water creatures and plant life, later to be
        returned to the pond. Can you find . . .

      - pondweeds

      - surface creatures, such as Water Striders or shiny
        black Whirligig Beetles

      - just-below-the-surface creatures (air breathers)
        such as Mosquito Larvae and Water Boatmen.

      - underwater creatures, such as Tadpoles (save in
        a jar of pond water for a week or two and see them
        hatch), Water Spiders, Copepods, and Water Mites.

      - creatures on the pondweeds and plants, such as
        the Dragonfly and Damselfly.

WATERSCOPE

Mat. - a relatively clear pond, lake, river, ocean, or bath tub.
- a medium-sized plastic bucket or tin can (Ie.-coffee can)
- <u>thick</u> plastic food wrap
- 1 large rubber band
- kitchen knife or can opener
- an adult supervisor!

Proc.- cut ends out of tin can, or cut a big circle out of bottom of bucket, with adult assistance.

- cover one end with a large piece of plastic wrap, and hold taut with rubber band, a few inches away from edge.

- press this end of waterscope into water to expose magnified plant life and water creatures below. (Leave open end above water.) Water pressure pushing up on the plastic forms a magnifying lens.

C8

ANTHILL IN A JAR

Mat. - 1 large clear glass jar with metal lid
- 1 tall skinny glass jar (or paper towel tube)
- loose or sandy soil
- 2 pieces of cheese cloth or nylon stocking
- ant trap (a little sugar water in a small jar or can)

Proc.- set skinny jar (or paper towel tube) upside-down in centre of large jar to leave no more than a 1 - 2 cm (1/2") space. Fill up space with soil, but don't pack too tightly.

- make a few tiny pin holes in lid to provide air.

- lay ant trap (see materials) on its side, preferably near an anthill.

- upon collecting about twenty ants (all from same colony to prevent feuding), place them on soil in jar and cap lid over two layers of netting.

- keep jar at room temperature in a dark location (or cover with dark cloth), and don't handle much.

- in a day or two, ants will begin to build a maze of tunnels and rooms in the soil!

ANTHILL IN A JAR continued . . .

- feed ants no more than twice a week with a few drops
  of sugar water, and maybe a few grains of birdseed
  sprinkled onto soil (or a few bits of rolled oats, cereal,
  bread crumbs, lettuce, or celery.) Don't overfeed!!

- Dribble a teaspoon or so of water onto soil at each
  feeding to prevent it from drying out.

- at end of project, return ants to <u>same</u> anthill.

DID YOU KNOW THAT ...

- some worker ants can carry up to 50x their weight!

- the queen, worker, and soldier ants are all female.
  The male ants mate and then die.

- a queen ant lays thousands of eggs in a lifetime.

- ants anaesthetize their prey with a squirt of acid.

- ants regurgitate food to feed each other.

WIGGLY WORMHOUSE

Mat. - large wide-mouthed jar
- equal amounts of damp (not wet) soil and sand
- worm food (Ie. grass clippings, potato peelings, leafy vegetables, celery or carrot tops, or small amount of coffee grounds).
- 2 pieces of cheesecloth or nylon stocking
- elastic band

Proc. - fill jar with equal layers of soil and sand, as shown, until 3/4 full. Pack down firmly.

- with a garden fork, dig in damp soil or compost heap to find two to four earthworms.

- lay earthworms on top of soil in jar, and cover with mesh held taut with elastic band. Place jar in cool, dark place.

- spray or sprinkle a little water on top of soil daily. Sprinkle on little bits of worm food every two or three days, if previous food is gone.

- apart from watering and feeding, handle jar very little, especially the first week.

- set your worm friends free before Fall. Can you see any baby worms?

Note - by using a red or green light for observing your worms, you may see more activity, such as worms pulling food into their burrow.

↳ DID YOU KNOW THAT . . .

- earthworms have no arms, legs, eyes, nose, ears, or teeth, but they have five hearts!!

- one acre of land contains about 2 - 3 million earthworms.

- earthworms help to enrich soil by digesting soil, and then casting off organic material.

- earthworms' greatest enemy is man (insecticides).

- earthworms mate on the soil surface at night.

- Australia has earthworms more than 3 metres long!!

- if an earthworm is cut in half, it can sometimes regrow lost parts. - - but don't try it !!!

Plant Your Own VEGETABLE GARDEN

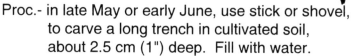

Mat. - 1 or 2 square metres of garden soil
- various packages of vegetable seeds
- garden hose or bucket of water
- stick or small shovel

Proc.- in late May or early June, use stick or shovel,
        to carve a long trench in cultivated soil,
        about 2.5 cm (1") deep. Fill with water.
- plant one type of seed in row, heeding the chart
  below.
- push soil back to fill trench. Pat down
  lightly, and spray well with water.
- now, dig another trench 30 - 40 cm (12-16") away
  planting a different type of seed, and so on.
- keep well-watered for first few weeks. After
  that, water well only once or twice a week.
- thin, when necessary, according to chart below.

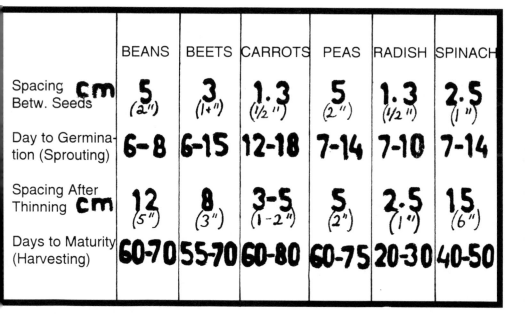

	BEANS	BEETS	CARROTS	PEAS	RADISH	SPINACH
Spacing cm Betw. Seeds	5 (2")	3 (1+")	1.3 (½")	5 (2")	1.3 (½")	2.5 (1")
Day to Germination (Sprouting)	6-8	6-15	12-18	7-14	7-10	7-14
Spacing After Thinning cm	12 (5")	8 (3")	3-5 (1-2")	5 (2")	2.5 (1")	15 (6")
Days to Maturity (Harvesting)	60-70	55-70	60-80	60-75	20-30	40-50

Grow a SUNFLOWER

Mat. - a few sunflower seeds
      - soil in a very sunny location

Proc. - in spring, poke a few holes in soil, 10 - 15 cm (4-6")
      apart and 1 - 2 cm (1/2") deep. Drop a seed into each
      one.

    - fill in holes and gently pat
      soil down. Lightly spray
      with water.

    - water often, and wait for seeds
      to sprout in about two weeks.

    - when sunflowers ripen, months later, (the backs will turn
      brownish yellow), cut the flowers off and leave them
      outside to dry for a few days. Then, remove black seeds.

TO ROAST SEEDS

    Spread seeds on a
cookie sheet. Add a little
vegetable oil and stir
well to coat seeds. Roast
at 300° F for about 25
minutes, or until crispy.
Sprinkle with salt.

CONSTELLATION CRAZE

Part.- 1 or more participants

Mat. - constellation chart below
      (or constellation book)

Proc.- on a dark night, preferably away from city
      lights, study the stars in the sky to find
      some well-known constellations. Some of
      the easiest to find are shown below. Do
      some research to learn about the legends
      associated with each constellation.

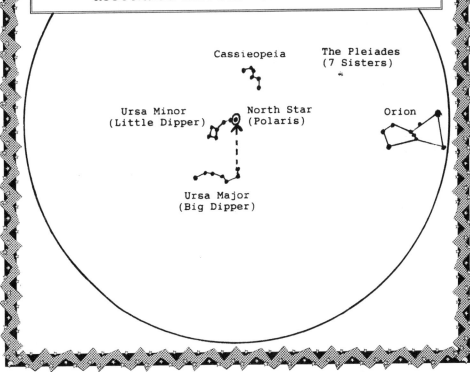

Cassieopeia

The Pleiades
(7 Sisters)

Ursa Minor
(Little Dipper)

North Star
(Polaris)

Orion

Ursa Major
(Big Dipper)

SNOWBALL SHOOTING RANGE

Part. - 1 or more participants

Mat. - tin cans or plastic bottles
   - sticky snow

Obj. - to earn points by hitting targets with snowballs.

Proc.- set up targets on a fence, wall, or
   step, away from any windows. Stack
   them to make a tower if you wish.

   - make a pile of snowballs.

   - standing behind a firing line 3 - 5 m (10-15') back,
   hurl snowballs at targets. Give yourself one
   point for each target hit.

   - the first player to reach ten points wins.

IGLOO BUILDING

Part. - 1 or more participants, including one adult!

Mat. - deep, firm snow that remains
       intact when an adult walks on it.
     - long kitchen knife

Proc.- stamp out a circle in the snow, about 6 - 7' wide.

- away from the circle, outline blocks in the snow with a stick, about 16" x 22", and 6" . Cut out with knife.

- carefully set blocks side by side around igloo circle. Trim top inner edge off so that next layer of blocks will lean slightly inward.

- with one person working from the inside, continue cutting, piling and trimming blocks, interspersing seams, until you have three or four layers all leaning inward. The last block to fill the hole at the top must be carefully cut and shaped to fit.

- cut out a door and crawl out.

- fill in all the cracks, inside and out, with snow.

- cut out a window hole if you wish.

Simple Version: Make snow bricks by packing moistened snow into bread pans. Trim and stack blocks to make a miniature igloo.

Make your own SKATING RINK

Mat. - large garden patch
- rake
- water hose with spray nozzle

Proc.- once ground has frozen over, rake top surface of garden
until as level and smooth as possible. Leave a 6-8 cm
(2-3") ridge of dirt all around outer edge, to hold water in.

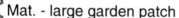

- on a freezing day (below $0°$ C) run hose on garden surface
for several hours, moving hose often so as not to collect
more than 2-3 cm (1") of water in one spot.

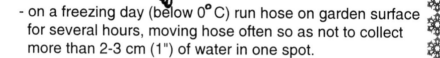

- every day, spray rink surface with more water to gradually
increase to desired thickness.

- if necessary, scrape with a snow shovel to smoothen.

"OUTDOOR ENCOUNTERS" LIST

WINTER ACTIVITIES

SNEAKY SNOWBALL FIGHT
  Hide behind a snow fort or snow hut built out of packed snow (or snow blocks made by pressing moist snow into bread pans). Then, make a pile of soft snowballs and start firing!

ICE SCULPTURE MAGIC
  Freeze water in an empty milk carton. Then, peel away cardboard and carefully chip away ice with a hammer and screw driver to create a unique sculpture.

SNUG SNOW HUT
  Pack down a big mound of snow. Leave overnight to freeze. Using a big shovel, carve out a doorway and hollow hut out.

SUMMER ACTIVITIES

SPRINKLER SPLASH
  On a hot day, cool off by running through your lawn sprinkler.

CHINESE BASEBALL
  Game is played the same as regular baseball except instead of a baseball the pitcher throws a large ball for the "batter" to kick.

FRISBEE BASEBALL
  Game is played the same as regular baseball except the "batter" just flings the Frisbee and then runs to the base/s.

PIG-IN-THE-MIDDLE
  Two or more players throw a Frisbee or kick a ball back and forth while the "pig" in the middle tries to intercept it, making the thrower (or kicker) the new "pig".

SUMMER OR WINTER ACTIVITIES

TEXTURE RUBBINGS
Remove the paper from a crayon. Then, rub the side of it onto a piece of paper held firmly against the bark of a tree, a leaf on the sidewalk, etc.

TAIL TUSSLE
Players tuck the end of a sock or washcloth into their pocket or pants, leaving a 15 cm (6") tail hanging out. Upon a signal, players triy to steal each other's tail. When only one person is left with a tail, the player with the most captured tails is the winner.

SQUASHED SARDINES
After counting to 100, players scatter to find the hidden "sardine", and then squeeze in to hide with him/her. Once all players are hiding together, the first person to have found the sardine becomes the new one.

KICK THE CAN
After kicking the tin can, players run and hide while the one chosen to be "It" retrieves the can. While trying to guard the can, "It" must try to spot hiding players, call out their names, and then beat them back to the can. If a "hider" kicks the can first, all captured players may go free again.

ANTI - I - OVER
A team member on one side of barn/building yells out "Anti-I-Over" and then throws the ball over the roof to the team on the other side. If the ball lands on the ground it's dead, but if it is caught, the receiver and his/her "guards" run around to touch the "base" on the other side of the building, without being tagged, choosing a prisoner to take back with him/her.

Introducing...

PARTNER CHALLENGE GAMES

THUMB WRESTLING

Part. - any number of pairs

Obj. - to be first to pin opponent's thumb to his/her hand for three seconds.

Proc.- face your opponent. Join right (or left) hands by hooking fingers.

- upon a signal, try to pin opponent's thumb to his/her hand for three seconds to win that round.

- the best of five rounds wins that series.

ARM WRESTLING

Part. - any number of partners

Mat. - a small table
- a strong arm!

Obj. - to be first to pull your opponent's arm down to the table.

Proc.- sitting across from opponent, with right (or left) elbows
on the table, lock hands. Your right arm must be
straight up and down, and your left arm must be
behind your back.

- upon a signal, try to pull your opponent's hand down
to table top, keeping your wrist straight. If your elbow
lifts from the table or your wrist touches the table, your
opponent automatically wins.

- winners may challenge other winners to determine the
"Champion Arm Wrestler".

LEG WRESTLING

Mat.   - any number of partners.

Obj.   - to be first to roll your opponent over backwards.

Proc. - partners lie side by side on their backs, arms hooked, facing opposite directions.

  - simultaneously, both players raise and lower their inside leg two times. On the third lift, players hook legs and try to roll each other over backwards.

  - the best of five rounds wins.

HUMAN TUG O' WAR

Part. - any number of partners

Mat. - a centre line, marked with any object
- a victory line, marked about four paces back
from both sides of centre line

Obj. - to pull your opponent back over victory line.

Proc.- partners face each other on opposite sides of
centre line, and hold onto each other's right
wrist (or left).

- upon a signal, each player tries to pull his/her
opponent back over victory line.

- winners may go on to challenge other winners.

Part. - 2 or more players

Mat. - broomstick or yardstick
     - 2 sturdy chairs
     - several thick books

Obj. - to shimmy under pole without knocking it down or falling over.

Proc.- balance pole between two chairs about 1 m (3') above ground, using books to adjust height.

- in turn, bend backwards and shimmy or wiggle your way underneath pole without knocking it off the books or falling over. Success at this height qualifies you to try the next height.

- after each player has had a turn at one height, remove one or two books from each side to lower pole a few inches

- the player who successfully shimmies under pole at the lowest height is the winner.

Part. - any number of partners

Mat. - 1 folded newspaper section each (or small mat)
 - 1 pillow each

Obj. - to be first to knock your opponent off his/her perch.

Proc. - partners stand on newspaper sections, facing each other.

 - without any body contact, partners swat each other with pillows to try to knock the other off his/her perch.

 - the first player to get knocked off loses the match.

BLOWBALL

Part. - 2 or more players

Mat. - 1 ping pong ball
 - kitchen or ping pong table

Obj. - to earn the most points by blowing ball off opponent's side of table.

Proc. - two teams stand on opposite sides of table.

 - without touching ball with any body part, players must blow to keep ping pong ball from falling off their team's side of table. If it does, or if ball touches a player, the opposing team scores a point.

 - the first team to score ten points is the winner of that match.

WATER-GUN SHOOT-OUT

Part. - 1 or more participants

Mat. - 3 plastic bottles each
   - 3 ping pong balls each
     (or empty film/medicine vials)
   - 1 water gun each

Proc.- stand up bottles on a wall,
       fence, box, or table.

   - set a ping pong ball (or vial)
     on top of each bottle.

   - stand behind a firing line 3 - 4 paces back.

   - upon the command "Draw!", players shoot
     water at their own targets.

   - the winner is the first player to knock off all
     three of his/her balls.

TWO SQUARE

Part.   - 2 players

Mat.   - a rubber playground ball
          - two adjacent sidewalk squares

Obj.   - to successfully serve and return the ball to be
          the first to earn 21 points.

Proc. - standing in or behind his/her square, the
          server bounces the ball once and then
          bats it into the adjacent square with an
          open hand.

     - the receiver lets it bounce once and then
       bats it back into the server's square, and so
       on.

     - if a player hits the ball on or outside of the
       line, fails to return a serve, or is hit by the
       ball, his/her opponent gains the serve, and
       also earns a point if he/she served that rally.

     - the first player to reach 21 points is the winner.

FOX and GEESE

Part. - 2 or more participants

Mat. - large, undisturbed bed of snow
- warm clothes and boots

Obj. - to avoid being tagged by the fox,
while staying on the boot tracks.

Proc.- stamp out a large, 8-spoked wagon wheel in the
the snow, about 14 paces across.

- to play, the "fox" stands in the middle, counts
aloud to ten, and then chases the "geese" along
the tracks. NO players may go off the paths.

- if a goose is tagged, he/she
lets out a loud yelp and
then becomes the new
fox.

WORD STAIRCASE

Part. - 2 or more

Mat. - 1 pencil/paper each

Obj. - to make the longest Word Staircase, beginning with the selected letter.

Proc.- ask a non-player to select a letter. (Not c, f, j, k, q, r, v, x, or z)

- players are given five minutes to make words beginning with the selected letter, starting with a two-letter word and increasing by one letter each time. Ie.

```
B
Be
Bib
Burn
Birds
Banana
Biscuit
Blisters
Blameless
```

- the player who builds the longest Word Staircase is the winner.

MEMORY MAZE

Part. - 2 - 4 players

Mat. - deck of number or picture cards

Obj. - to match and collect the most pairs.

Proc.- choose 12 - 14 matched pairs from deck.

- shuffle cards, and lay them out, face down, as shown.

- in turn, each player turns over two cards to see if they match. If not, both cards are replaced, but if they do match, the player keeps the pair and takes another turn.

- when the cards are all gone, the player with the most pairs wins.

SPEED!

Part. - 2 players

Mat. - deck of number cards

Obj. - to be the first to play out all your cards.

Proc.- two piles of six cards each are placed face-down
in centre. Remainder of deck is dealt to two
players, who each pick up five of those cards for
their hand.

- simultaneously, players flip the top card of a
centre pile and quickly play any cards from their
hand that are one number higher or lower
(or the highest/lowest cards may be matched).

- players take more cards from their stack to
always maintain a hand of five cards. When no
one can play, two more centre cards are flipped.

- the first one to play out is the winner.

CHEAT

Part.- 2 - 7 players

Mat. - deck of number cards

Obj. - to play out all your cards.

Proc.- deal all cards to players, face down.

- player on dealer's left starts the game by placing a card/s face-down in the centre, and calling out "two ones", or whatever amount is laid. The next player calls out out "twos" and so on.

- a player may "cheat" by placing incorrect cards down if he/she has none of the assigned number, or to just slough some cards off. However, if someone calls "cheat", the offending player must collect all the cards in the centre.

- if someone calls "cheat" on an "innocent" player, the caller must collect all the cards in the centre.

- the first person to successfully play out is the winner.

CRAZY EIGHTS

Part. - 2 or more players

Mat. - deck of number cards

Obj. - to be the first to play out all your cards.

Proc.- deal seven cards to each player. Place
remaining pile in centre, flipping over
top card.

- player on dealer's left starts by laying a
card of the same value <u>or</u> suit on top of
flipped card.

- "8's" are wild cards, and may be played
at any time. The one who lays it chooses
the suit for the next player to follow.

- anyone unable to play must keep drawing
from centre pile until he/she <u>can</u> play.
(If cards run out, shuffle discard pile and
use again.)

- the first person to play out is the winner.

BASEBALL
ADDITION/SUBTRACTION [2]

Part. - 1 - 4 players

Mat. - deck of number cards
     - 1 pencil/paper each

Obj. - to be first to win nine "innings" by adding up the
       largest sums.

Proc.- each player takes four cards from
     the pile and assembles them to
     add up to the largest sum possible.
     Use paper or chalkboard to add up.

$$\begin{array}{r} 5\ 2 \\ +\ 4\ 3 \\ \hline 9\ 5 \end{array}$$

    - the player with the highest sum wins that "inning".

    - continue with four new cards each. The first
     player to win nine innings wins the game.

Note - In "Baseball Subtraction", the player with the lowest
       answer wins that inning.

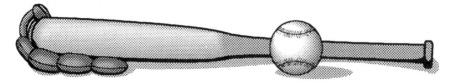

RACE TO 100

Part. - 2 or 3 players

> A fun way to practice
> "PLACE VALUE" skills!

Mat. - 1 die each
- 100 Lego or Duplo cubes each (or paper/pencils)

Obj. - to be first to shake die to add up cubes
(or pencil ticks) to reach exactly 100.

Proc.- in turn, or simultaneously for more excitement,
each player shakes die and takes that number
of cubes (or records that amount of pencil ticks).

- each player joins his/her cubes together
(or draws a line through ticks) each time he/she
has enough to make a "ten".

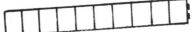

- the first player to add up his/her cubes (or ticks)
to exactly 100 is the winner.

Part. - 2 - 4 players

Mat. - deck of number cards

Obj. - to win the most rounds (cards) by flipping the highest card.

Proc.- deal out all the cards.

- simultaneously, each player flips the top card of his/her pile. The one with the highest card wins all the cards in that round. In the case of a tie for the highest card, those involved flip again.

- when all the cards in the piles are gone, the player with the most cards win.

Note - for a change, you may also play that the lowest card wins.

MULTIPLICATION WAR (or ADDITION)

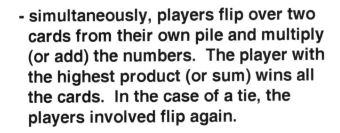

> ## Three games to make MATH DRILLS more fun!

Part. - 1 - 3 players

Mat. - deck of cards, numbers 1 - 10

Obj. - to win the most rounds (cards) by having the highest product (or sum).

Proc.- shuffle and deal out all the cards.

- simultaneously, players flip over two cards from their own pile and multiply (or add) the numbers. The player with the highest product (or sum) wins all the cards. In the case of a tie, the players involved flip again.

- after the piles are gone, the winner is the one with the most cards.

Variation - only two cards are flipped from two piles of cards in the centre. The first player to call out the correct product (or sum) wins those cards.

Variation - to work on a specific number family, multiply flipped card by a selected number card placed in the centre.

"PARTNER CHALLENGE" LIST

TABLETOP HOCKEY
Place heavy books around edges of a table to form a rink (or tape cardboard strips around edge), leaving a gap for goals. Then, use Popsicle sticks or spoon handles for hockey sticks and a wad of paper for a puck.

SCOOP BALL
Make ball scoops by cutting two or more 1-litre (or 1-quart) plastic milk jugs in half horizontally. Toss a small ball back and forth to a partner, using only the scoop to catch and throw.

SLAPPER!
Hold your open hands face up while your partner holds his/hers face-down above yours. Then, sporadically jerk your hands out and over to try to slap the back of your partner's hands before he/she can pull them away. After ten tries, switch roles.

PAIR - IT [4]
In turn, players shake one die and take that number of cards from the deck, setting down any matching pairs. When the deck of cards is gone, the winner is the one with the most pairs.

SHOE KICK
Line up at starting line. Upon a signal, kick off a loose, untied shoe as far as you can. The owner of the furthest shoe wins.

CRAZY CARPET WALK
With two pieces of carpet or folded newspaper each, race to the finish line, only stepping on carpet (or newspaper), placed one in front of the other.

RAINY DAY FUN

Why not go inside and...

WACKY WINDOWS

Mat. - 1 Tbsp. tempera paint powder
  (from craft/teacher's store or stationer)
  - 1 Tbsp. liquid dish soap
  - paintbrush
  - old towel

Proc.- mix powder paint and liquid soap together.

  - cover windowsill with towel to protect it.

  - with permission from a parent, paint faces, flowers, butterflies, etc. on kitchen or bedroom window.

  - store extra paint in sealed container.

  - to clean, wash off paint with wet rag.

HOME-MADE FACEPAINT

INGREDIENTS
1 Tbsp. shortening, at room temp.
  (or 1 Tbsp. thick handcream)
15 or more drops food coloring
  (or paint/Kool-Aid/Jell-o powder
  mixed with a drop or two of water)
1 - 2 Tbsp. cornstarch

METHOD
  Mix well, gradually adding
cornstarch to make a thick paste.
Make various colors, and store in
sealed container in fridge. Use to
decorate faces at birthday parties,
for Hallowe'en, or just for fun!

HOME-MADE FABRIC PAINT

Mix food coloring or Kool-Aid powder into small bottles of white glue. Sqeeze glue onto paper or fabric to make puffy designs. Color will darken as it dries.

HOME-MADE BATHTUB CRAYONS

INGREDIENTS
2 - 3 tsp. paint powder dissolved in 1 T. water
2 tsp. glycerine
3/4 C. Ivory Soap Flakes

METHOD
In a small bowl, whip together ingredients until thick and crumbly. Roll into crayon shapes. Let dry for a day or two. Make different colors. To clean bathtub walls, wipe with a rag, or try spraying off with a spray bottle or water gun.

SHADOW PUPPETS

Mat. - a clear wall
   - table lamp
   - heavy paper or thin cardboard
   - animal or people cookie cutters or magazine pictures
   - scissors and tape
   - hole punch (opt.)
   - straws or Popsicle sticks

Proc.- trace cookie cutters or glue magazine pictures onto cardboard (or draw your own animal or people shapes).
   - cut out and punch holes (or poke with a pencil) to make eyes, ears, mouth, etc.
   - tape straws or Popsicle sticks onto back of shapes.
   - in a dark room, shine light from behind puppets so they cast a shadow on the wall. Perform skits with your puppets.

SHADOW SHAPES

Mat. - a clear wall
- 1 table lamp or flashlight

Proc. - in a dark room, shine light from behind you onto a clear wall.

- hold your hands as shown to make animal shadows on the wall.

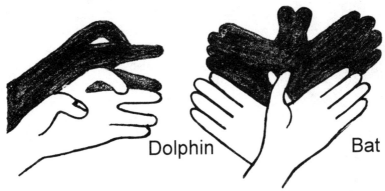

Dolphin   Bat

- move your fingers to make ears wiggle, wings flap, mouths open and close, etc.

- can you invent your own shadow shapes?

Make Your Own Dollhouse

MAT. - 2 identical boxes, about 38 x 21 cm
        (15x8"), such as a 9-pack Kleenex box
        (or ask your dad to build one out of wood)
- carpet and/or linoleum scraps
- wallpaper scraps or wrapping paper
- glue and heavy tape

PROC.- cut off flaps and glue boxes together.
     Secure with heavy tape.
- enclose front rough edges with tape.
- glue carpet or linoleum to "floors".
- glue wallpaper onto walls.

IDEAS FOR DOLLHOUSE FURNITURE/UTENSILS

Table - small lid glued onto large thread spool

Stools - small painted thread spools

Fridge/Stove - small boxes painted appropriately

Couch/Bed - pieces of foam covered with
        fabric and glued together

Dresser - matchstick box cut/folded in half
        and glued. Use split pins for handles.

Lamps - small cupcake liners glued onto
        thread spool or coiled pipecleaner

Mirror - unwrinkled tin-foil glued into baby
        food jar lid or onto cardboard piece

Wallhangings - small photos or magazine
        pictures glued into small lids

Broom - long grass glued and tied   **Step1**   **Step2**
        onto bottom end of 1/8" dowel

Dishes - tiny, plastic butter/jam containers, bottle
        caps, walnut shells, tiny lids (Ie.Lypsol lids)

Food - make tiny bread loaves, buns,
        apples, bananas, etc. using
        Bread Dough Art recipe in
        "Arts & Crafts" section. Paint,
        or spread a little glue on and
        sprinkle with poppy/sesame/
        caraway seeds or cornmeal.

Grow Your Own Yummy
BEAN SPROUTS

MATERIALS
- glass jar (1 qt. size)
- 1 Tbsp. small beans/seed (ie. alfalfa) or 3 Tbsp. large beans (ie. lentils, mung, or raw sunflower seeds)
- clean cheesecloth or mesh
- elastic band

METHOD
- measure beans into jar, and fill with water. Cover with mesh and secure with elastic.

- soak overnight, or until beans plump up (no more than 6 hours for sunflower seeds).

- drain water through mesh. Rinse and drain again. Place jar on side in warm, dark place.

- rinse daily, draining well to prevent molding.

- when nicely sprouted after 3 or 4 days (6 - 7 for alfalfa), eat as a healthy snack, or in a salad, sandwich, or stir-fry dish. Store extra bean sprouts in sealed container in fridge.

MATERIALS

- 1 pint glass jar with lid
- 1/2 pint whipping cream
- 1 clean marble (opt.)
- 1/2 tsp. salt (opt.)

Make your *own* BUTTER

METHOD

- pour whipping cream into jar and add washed marble. Shake jar continuously and vigorously, while you chant the following verse. Then, switch off with someone else.

Verse: Shake it and shake it, the marble and the cream,
Shake it and shake it 'til the butter can be seen.

- after ten minutes or so, when the marble stops "hopping around", remove marble and drain buttermilk off.

- mix in salt, and serve on crackers or bread.

POP-UP BOOKS

Mat. - 9 x 12" (23x30 cm) construction paper
- scissors and glue
- crayons or felt markers

Proc.- fold paper in half. Cut two
3.5 cm (1.5") slits in fold, about
8 cm (3") from each side edge.

- push middle tab through opening,
and crease it on the inside of card.

- open up card, and glue picture onto
pop-up tab. Add a background
scene, if you wish.

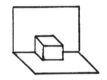

- if making a card, just add a cover. If making a book,
glue several similar pages together and add a cover.

OTHER BOOK IDEAS

Round Book   - draw/write on paper plates held together
with curtain ring or pipe cleaner.

Accordian Book - fold long strip of paper "accordian-style".
Glue cover onto first and last pages.

Bound Book   - cover cardboard rectangle with fabric, turning
edges in. Fold a few slightly smaller sheets
in half. With needle and heavy thread, sew
paper and cover together along paper crease.

Fun Ways to Improve Your READING SKILLS

READ! READ! READ!

Every chance you get, read books that interest you. It may be mysteries, hockey books, or even comics! - - or save your money and subscribe to your favorite children's magazine! For oral reading practice, read often to a parent, sibling, or even the family dog!

LISTEN TO YOURSELF

Using lots of expression, read a favorite story on tape. Ring a bell when it's time to turn the page. Listen to the tape often, as you follow along in the book.

CLOZE

Ask a parent or sibling to cover every fifth word in a story. (Post-It Notes work well.) Then, read the story, using context clues to predict what the blank words might say.

MESSAGE MANIA

Make print meaningful! Using paper, chalkboard, or whiteboard, frequently record little notes, messages, reminders, etc. back and forth to family members.

WILD WORD PACKS

Record "trouble words" on recipe/computer cards or cardboard strips. Read them often to an experienced reader. Mark card with a star for each word read correctly on separate occasions. Three stars on a card entitles you to remove it from the pack.

WORD BREAKDOWN

Break down difficult words into parts to make them easier to decode.
(le. Compound Words - jump/rope, Affixes - un/happy, help/less, or Syllables - re/luc/tant)

CRAZY QUIPS

On 24 strips of paper, record six names (le. George Washington), six action words (le. burped), six places (le. on the moon), and six time periods (le. last night, in 1942). Then, use a strip from each group to build crazy sentences. Read them out to someone else.

PARTNER TALES

On paper, write a few sentences to begin an exciting story. Then, pass it to a partner to add a few more, and so on. Be sure to carefully read what your partner writes so the sentences you add will make sense.

READING SKILLS continued . . .

BAKE UP A STORM!
Practice your reading skills by following a recipe to make something yummy!

BE A COMIC
Alone or with a partner, read a comic as a play. Change your voice for each character.

MIXED-UP COMICS
Cut out each "box" in a comic strip, and mix them all up. Then, read them carefully to enable you to put them back in the correct order.

TUNE IN ON TAPES
Listen to a story tape as you follow along in the book. - - or, sing a favorite song as you follow the words in a songbook.

BUILD SKILLS
Purchase fun Reading Comprehension workbooks at a bookstore or department/ grocery store.

NIGHTLY NOVEL
Ask a parent or older sibling if they will read one chapter of a novel to you each night. This will help you to develop an ear for book language and a love for reading!

GET TACTILE !

Find as many tactile ways of practicing "trouble words" as possible. For instance, use fingerpaint, playdough, brown sugar sprinkled onto a cookie sheet, or a wet paintbrush on chalkboard or sidewalk to practice spelling words. - - or print them onto someone's back with your finger for them to guess what you spelled!

DICTIONARY DETECTIVE

In alphabetical order in a scribbler, record one letter of the alphabet in the top corner of each page. Each time you want to know how to spell a word, look for it in your "Spelling Dictionary". If it's not there yet, ask someone to help you record it on the correct page.

JOURNAL JOY

Each day, use mostly your own spelling to write to a parent or older sibling in a scribbler or diary. Hopefully, he/she will write back to you, using and correctly spelling a _few_ of your misspelled words. You can only learn a few at a time!

SPELLING SKILLS continued . . .

IN REVERSE
Proof-read your stories, letters, etc. from back to front. This deters you from focusing on the meaning, making spelling errors more apparent.

WORD-FAMILY FUN
Learn to spell words in related groups or families by just changing the first letter to make many different words. (Ie. b[ar], c[ar], f[ar], etc.)

HANGMAN HYSTERIA
Frequently play Hangman, using words you are having trouble spelling.

GAIN WITH GAMES
Play simple board games that help to improve your spelling, such as Junior Scrabble, Probe, Boggle, etc.

WORDSEARCH WIT
Make your own Wordsearches and Crossword Puzzles using "trouble words". Trade puzzles with a friend.

BUILD SKILLS
Work on fun spelling workbooks purchased from a bookstore or department/grocery store.

Fun Ways to Improve Your WRITING SKILLS

1. WINNING WRITING PROGRAM

When writing a story, carefully go through the following steps:

A. CHOOSE A TOPIC
- brainstorm for a list of ideas, research, talk to others, or look at books, magazines, and photo albums to get ideas for a writing topic.

B. ROUGH DRAFT
- make a story outline, as follows:

Beginning	Middle	End
Who? Where? When? What?	Problem	How problem gets solved.

- begin writing, double-spaced to leave room for editing.

- don't worry about spelling yet. Just circle difficult words and keep your thoughts flowing!

C. REVISE AND EDIT, as shown:

--- Cross out unnecessary or confusing information.
∧ Add information.
⤸ Move parts around.
Improve vocabulary (Ie. He ran. raced)
Correct (spelling) and grammar (Ie. he are is)
Correct punctuation (. , ? !)
Correct capitalization (Tim)
Improve paragraph/indentation placement. (P).

E15

WRITING SKILLS continued . . .

D. RESPOND
- listen to your story being read, as is, by someone else. Would any changes improve your story? Can the reader give you any suggestions?

E. PUBLISH
- write a good copy, perhaps in book form, or type it onto a computer using a graphics (picture) program.

F. SHARE
- read your story to others, using good expression.

- display it or hang it up for others to enjoy.

- record your story on tape.

- make character puppets and perform a puppet play.

- do art work, such as paintings, murals, collages, clay work, etc. related to your story.

- wrap your book up and give it away for a special gift.

- send your story to a magazine publisher or book club who publishes children's work.

2. WRITE! WRITE! WRITE!

Use every opportunity to practice your writing skills! For instance:

- keep "Shopping Lists", "Job Lists", etc.

- leave cheery messages for family and friends on bulletin/white boards, lunch bags, etc.

- make and send a thank you card to someone, in appreciation for a special gift or act of kindness.

- write a letter to a faraway relative or friend.

- send a riddle, a question, or a story about yourself to Owl or Chickadee magazine.

- write to Ann Landers or Abby for some advice.

- find a book from a library or bookstore that lists free things for kids. Write to the addresses recorded to get some free stuff!

- express your thoughts, feelings, and ideas in a daily journal described on the next page.

JOURNAL FUN

Mat. - a diary or school scribbler
- a pencil or pen

Proc.- begin keeping a daily or weekly diary/journal. Use some of the following topic ideas, if you wish.

TOPIC IDEAS

1) Last night (or last summer), I . . .
2) When I grow up, I . . .
3) I love . . .
4) If I could fly, I would . . .
5) Sometimes I'm afraid of . . .
6) I laughed so hard when . . .
7) When I was little, I . . .
8) My best friend is . . .
9) If I was invisible, I would . . .
10) If I had three wishes, I would wish for . . .
11) It really upsets me when . . .
12) I'm really good at . . .
13) I would love to meet . . .
14) If I had a million dollars, I would . . .
15) I was so embarrassed when . . .
16) If I was a school principal, I would . . .
17) For my next birthday, I would like . . .

"RAINY DAY FUN" LIST

FOR THE BIRDS
With a needle and thread, string popcorn to hang on trees for hungry birds to enjoy.

TOOTHPICK ARCHITECTURE
Build bridges, towers, buildings, etc. out of toothpicks joined together with wads of playdough or chewing gum.

GEO - DESIGNS
Using cardboard tracers of the following shapes, draw and cut out 8 - 10 of each shape out of heavy paper. (Colored is nice.) Use these shapes to create unique pictures and designs. Then, trace the results onto paper.

SILLY PUTTY
Mix together 4 tsp. white glue, 3 Tbsp. cornstarch, and food coloring. Add more of either ingredient to get desired consistency. Then, squeeze, pull, poke, and roll putty.

TRICKY TOE PICS
With a crayon, felt marker, or paintbrush held between your toes, try to draw pictures on paper taped to the floor.

FIZZLE FUN
Pour 1/4 C. vinegar into a pop bottle and 2 tsp. baking soda into a balloon. Stretch open end of balloon over bottle opening, shaking soda into bottle. What happens?

FORTUNE FANTASY

Fold a square piece of paper to make a fortune teller. (Fold corners to centre. Flip over and repeat step. Then, fold in half and spread open ends to make a pyramid.) Record numbers on the outside, colors on the inside, and exciting fortunes under the flaps.

TAPE TALES

Record yourself on tape as you impart some corny jokes, a crazy weather forecast, or a nutty news broadcast regarding the events in a well-known fairy tale. Listen to yourself as you play it back.

SILLY SKITS

Practice acting out simple fairy tales or stories. Add props, and perform them for family and friends.

SUPER STRING GAMES

Borrow a book from the library to learn how to do "Cat's Cradle" and other fun string games.

GAMES GALORE

Play simple board/card games such as Pit, Yahtzee, Monopoly, Pictionary, Sorry, Bingo, Fish, Double Soitaire, etc.

CITRUS FRUIT PLANTS

Soak a few orange, grapefruit, lemon, or pomegranate seeds overnight. Press seeds about 5 cm (2") into bug-free soil in plant pot. Fill in holes, and water well. Place in sunny spot and water when dry. Seeds will sprout in about two weeks.

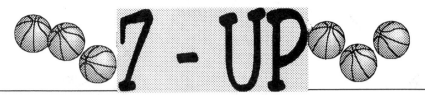

7 - UP

Part. - play alone, or race with a friend

Mat. - rubber ball or tennis ball
     - windowless wall adjacent to sidewalk or
      concrete compound

Obj. - to successfully complete all 21 ball routines.

Proc.- do the following ball activities according to the
       number listed.

ONESIES
7X - throw ball against wall and catch it.
6X - throw ball against wall, let it bounce once, and
     then catch it.
5X - bounce ball.
4X - angle-throw ball against the ground so it
     bounces up against wall. Catch it.
3X - throw ball high on wall and touch ground. Catch
     it before it bounces.
2X - throw ball against wall and touch ground. Catch
     it after one bounce.
1X - throw ball in air and touch ground. Catch it
     before it bounces.

    Repeat complete routine adding one of the
following "tricks" each time through.

TWOSIES   - throw ball under leg for each routine.
THREESIES - clap once after each throw.
FOURSIES - twirl around after each clap.

JUMP BALL

Part. - at least 4 players

Mat. - 1 bouncy ball
- a windowless wall next pavement.

Obj. - to work your way to the front of the line by successfully jumping the ball.

Proc. - players spread out, one behind the other, in front of a wall.

- the front player tosses the ball against the wall and jumps over it on the first bounce.

- the next player jumps over it on the second bounce,and so on down the line.

- a player who misses the jump or who is touched by the ball must go to the end of the line, and the game continues.

Along-the-Wall DODGE BALL

Part. - 4 or more players

Mat. - soft ball (ie. inflatable)
- windowless wall

Obj. - to side-step along the wall to avoid being hit by the ball.

Proc.- players stand in front of wall, about 1 m (2-3') apart. Mark boundaries about 1 m from outside players.

- standing about 4.5 m (15') from wall, the "shooter" throws the ball at players, who side-step to try to dodge the ball. Anyone hit is eliminated.

- the last "dodger" left becomes the new shooter.

FOUR SQUARE

Part. - 4 players
(or more, if spares replace players who go out.)

Mat. - chalk
- 1 rubber playground ball
- concrete compound

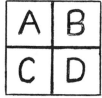

Obj. - to work your way to "Square A" by successfully
returning the ball, and by putting fellow-players out.

Proc.- with chalk, draw four joined squares on pavement, about
1 1/2 m (5'x5') each, and label them A, B, C, and D.

- each player stands in the far corner of each square.
The player in "Box A" starts the game by bouncing the
ball once and then batting it into another square with an
open hand.

- the receiver must let it bounce once in his/her square,
and then bat it into another square, and so on.

- if a player hits the ball on or outside of the line, fails to
return a serve, or is hit by the ball, he/she must move to
"Square D" while the other players move up.

GUARDED GATE

Part. - 6 - 10 players

Mat. - 1 mid-sized ball

Obj. - to prevent ball from passing through through your open legs.

Proc. - players stand in a circle with their legs apart.

- a "pitcher" stands inside the circle and tries to roll the ball between a player's legs.

- players in the circle try to stop the ball with their hands or knees (feet may not move), and then roll it back to the pitcher.

- if the ball passes through a player's legs, he/she becomes the new pitcher.

BLACKBEARD'S BOOTY

Part.- 4 or more players

Mat. - treasure (Ie. beanbag or pencil case)

Obj. - to steal "Blackbeard's Booty" without being tagged.

Proc.- the person chosen to be be Blackbeard stands
        guard over his/her jewels, while the remaining
        players form a circle around.

    - players try to steal the treasure from Blackbeard
      without being tagged, as this results in elimination.

    - you may help each other by teasing the roaring
      pirate away from his/her jewels, or even resorting
      to a mass charge, if nothing else works.

    - the player who captures the treasure, untagged,
      becomes the new pirate.

TWOS AND THREES

Part. - at least 8

Obj. - to avoid being caught by the cat before joining the circle again.

Proc.- partners of two or three stand one behind the other in the formation of a circle.

- one "cat" chases a "mouse" in and around the circle, switching roles if the mouse is caught.

- to gain safety, or for a rest, the mouse (or cat) may quickly stand in front of one of the pairs, and the back person becomes the new mouse (or cat).

SLAP and RUN

Part. - at least 8 players

Obj. - to avoid being captured by tagging the "scout" before he/she makes it "home".

Proc.- teams line up on opposite sides of the playing area, about 25 paces apart, facing each other.

- the first player in one line-up (the scout) runs to the other line-up, whose players all have their hands held out, facing downward.

- the scout runs along the line-up, slapping each one's hands from underneath. However, when he/she slaps someone's hands from above, that player must chase the scout back home.

- if the scout makes it back safely, the chaser must join that team. Both runners go to the end of the line. However, if the scout is tagged before crossing the team line, he/she must join onto the end of the opposition line-up.

- now, the second team sends a scout, and so on.

- the game ends when there are no players left on one side.

  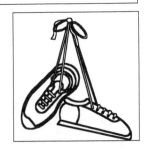

TAG GAMES

BALL TAG

Players are tagged by being hit with a soft ball (Ie. foam or ping pong ball) below the neck. Three hits means you're "frozen". The last player frozen is "it".

"DOCTOR, DOCTOR" TAG

Players who are tagged must keep a hand on the spot touched (Ie.- arm, back, or foot). Three tags means you're frozen. The last player frozen is "it".

BLOB TAG

When players are tagged, they must join hands with the "Blob" and help chase. When the Blob grows to include four players, it splits in half to make two blobs. The last player tagged becomes the new "Blob".

SHADOW TAG

Playing on a sunny day, players are frozen when the "Jinx" steps on their shadow and calls out "Jinx!" They can only be unfrozen if a free player jumps on their shadow five times. Three times jinxed and a player must sit out. The last free player becomes the next "Jinx".

PARACHUTE GAMES

Part.- 6 - 30 players, depending on size of parachute.

Mat. - school parachute (or large, light blanket or sheet)
    - 1 light ball (Ie. inflatable)

JAWS!
"Jaws" crawls around underneath the parachute, while
remaining players stand around the outer edge, flapping it.
(No peeking underneath.) If someone's legs are grabbed
by "Jaws" he/she must let out a blood-curdling scream, and
then crawl underneath to become another shark. The last
player left still standing becomes the new "Jaws".

POPCORN
Players stand around the parachute, with two teams on opposite
sides. A ball is placed in the centre. Upon the count of three,
players try to flip or bounce the ball off opponent's side of the
parachute, earning a point for his/her team.

CAT AND MOUSE
One "cat" crawls around on top of the parachute (no shoes on),
while one or two "mice" scurry around underneath. Meanwhile, the
remaining players kneel around the parachute, flapping wildly to
help conceal the mice. If a mouse is "pounced on", he/she chooses
a new cat, and then joins the "flappers". The cat now becomes a
mouse, and the game continues.

BIRTHDAYS
Players stand around parachute and hold onto the edge.
Any players whose birth month is called out by the "caller" must
run underneath the parachute and escape out through the other
side, without getting trapped.

Marble Game
-RINGER-

Part. - 2 or more players

Mat. - chalk
   - 5 - 7 marbles each

Firing Line

Obj. - to capture the most marbles by knocking
   them out of the ring.

Proc. - on pavement, draw a circle, about
   1/2 - 1 m (2 - 3') in diameter.

- players place an equal number of marbles
  inside the circle, at least 5 cm (2") apart.

- from a firing line about 1 m (3'+) from edge of
  circle, take turns shooting a marble at target
  marbles to knock them them out of the ring.

- if you shoot a marble out, keep that marble
  <u>and</u> your shooter, and take another turn. If
  your unsuccessful shooter remains inside of
  the circle, it becomes a target marble.

- the player who captures the most marbles is
  the winner. Play for keeps or just for fun.

Marble Game
- POTSY -

Part. - 2 or more players

Mat. - 5 marbles each

Obj. - to be the first to shoot all five of your marbles into the pot.

Proc.- dig a small hole ("pot") in the ground with your heel.

- from a starting line drawn about 2 m (6') back, take turns trying to shoot one of your marbles into the "pot".

- the first player to shoot all five of his/her marbles in is the winner. If you are playing for keeps, the winner gets to keep all of the marbles in the pot.

Marble Game
-STRADDLES-

Part. - 2 players

Mat. - about 20 marbles each

Obj. - to be the first to capture (hit) all *five of* your opponent's target marbles.

Proc.- sit it straddle position, facing your partner, about 2 m (6'+) apart. Each of you places five marbles inside your straddle, at least 5 cm (2") apart.

- take turns shooting a marble to hit one or more of your opponent's marble/s. If you are successful, you may claim that marble/s and your shooter and take another turn. If you are unsuccessful, you must forfeit your shooter and your turn.

- the first player to capture all five of opponent's marbles is the winner.

HOPSCOTCH

Part.- 2 or more players

Mat. - chalk
  - 1 marker each (Ie.-stone or chain)

Obj. - to be first to successfully toss
  marker and hop through all
  Hopscotch squares.

Proc.- using chalk, draw a Hopscotch grid on sidewalk as shown,
  each square about 35 x 35 cm (14" x 14").

- in turn, players toss their marker into Square #1, hop over
  that square, and continue down the grid to the end and
  back, spinning around on Squares 9 and 10.

- upon returning to Square #2, players pick up their marker,
  while still on one foot, and hop out of the grid, Then, they
  toss their marker to Square #2, and repeat the sequence,
  hopping over marker squares both coming and going.

- players forfeit their turn when their marker is tossed <u>on</u>
  or <u>outside</u> the line (marker must be returned to previous
  square), players step on a line or into any square with a
  marker in it, or players fall down or touch a single square
  with both feet.

- the winner is the first one to successfully toss marker and
  hop through all of the squares on the grid.

F14

CHINESE SKIPPING

Part. - 3 or more players

Mat. - 1 elastic jump-rope (a continuous rope, about 2 m (6')
      long, made by looping many elastic bands together.

Obj. - to successfully perform jump sequence at each level.

Proc.- two players hold the rope taut with their ankles,
      forming a long, rectangular box.

  - the jumper hops in the following sequence (or you
    may make up your own sequence).

1 - jump into box
2 - jump out, stradding both strands
3 - jump to straddle one side
4 - jump to straddle the other side
5 - jump into box again
6 - jump out to straddle both strands again
7 - jump on both strands, pinning it to the ground
8 - let elastic go and lift your leg out

  - when all jumpers have had a turn at ankle level, rope
    is moved up to next level (Ie. knees, thighs, waist,
    and armpits) for successful players. Any who make
    a mistake must become an "ender".

Variation: with three enders, the sequence is as follows:
    1 - jump in and out all around the triangle
    2 - jump <u>on</u> rope, on three sides and back "home"
       again, without jumping in or outside of triangle
    3 - repeat Step #1 hopping on only one foot
    4 - repeat Step #2 hopping on only one foot

F15

SENSATIONAL SKIPPING

SINGLE SKIPPING TRICKS AND VERSES

Pepper Step - skip pepper on one foot, two feet, or on alternate feet.

Doubles - turn the rope very fast so it passes under your feet twice for each jump.

Backwards - skip while turning rope backwards.

Cross-Overs - cross your arms and jump through "crossed over" rope on every second jump.

ABC Skipping - skip vinegar as you call out names of people or countries beginning with each consecutive letter of the alphabet.

TINKER TAILOR

Skip vinegar (normal speed) to:

Jump rope, jump rope, tell me true

1. Whom will I be married to?
   Tinker, tailor, soldier, sailor
   Rich man, poor man, beggerman, thief,
   Doctor, lawyer, Tribal Chief . . .
   (Skip pepper, chanting list repeatedly, until you trip.)
2. To my wedding, what will I wear?
   Silk, satin, cotton baton . . .
3. What kind of ring will I wear?
   Diamond, ruby, ten-cent ring . . .
4. What kind of house will we have?
   Castle, mansion, pig pen . . .
5. How many children will we have?
   1, 2, 3 . . .   (Traditional)

GROUP SKIPPING VERSES

HELP!!

Enders turn rope at normal speed, and then gradually speed up to pepper, chanting "H", "E", "L", "P" in time to the rope. When the jumper trips on a letter, he/she must skip according to the list below to see what number he/she can reach. Try to beat each other's records.

H - "Highwire" - rope doesn't touch the ground.
E - "Eyes"   - eyes must be kept closed.
L - "Lollipop" - twirl around after each jump.
P - "Pepper"   - jump to rope turned very fast!

(Unknown)

DUTCH GIRL

One or two jumpers skip vinegar (normal speed) while following the directions in the verse.

I'm a little Dutch girl dressed in blue.
Here are the actions I must do.
Salute to the captain, bow to the queen.
Turn right around and count to sixteen.
1, 2, 3, 4 . . .
(Skip pepper to numbers until you trip. Take another turn if you make it successfully to "16")

(Traditional)

GROUP SKIPPING/DOUBLE DUTCH VERSES

BUMPER CAR

One or two jumpers skip vinegar (normal speed) to:
Had a little bumper car in 1948.
Burned around the co-o-o-o-o-orner.
 (Jump out, run around enders, and jump back in.)
Slammed on the brakes.
Policeman caught me, put me in jail.
All I got was ginger ale.
How many bottles did I drink?
10, 20, 30 . . .
 (Skip pepper until you trip on a number.)
Note: It's bad luck to land on 100!

(Traditional)

TWO LITTLE DICKIE BIRDS

Two jumpers skip vinegar (normal speed) to:
Two little dickie birds sitting on the wall.
One named Peter, one named Paul.
Fly away Peter (one skipper jumps out)
Fly away Paul (the other skipper jumps out)
Come back when your initial's called.
A, B, C . . . (or age, birth month, birth date, etc.)
 (If a player trips on the rope, he/she becomes an ender.)

(Traditional)

"RECESS ROMP" LIST

ACTIVE GAMES

CHICKEN FIGHT CHALLENGE
  Each pair of piggybacking "chickens" tries to bump or pull an opponent off his/her partner's back. The last pair still intact wins.

FRISBEE FOOTBALL
  Played the same as regular football, except there are no downs, no travelling with the Frisbee, and players score by throwing the Frisbee to a team-mate standing behind the goal line.

SHOE STEW
  A group of players removes and piles their shoes together, 15 - 20 paces away from the fence. Upon a signal, players race to find their shoes, tie them on, and then be first to make it back to the fence.

CROWS AND CRANES
  Two teams, the "Crows" and the "Cranes", face each other on centre line. When the leader calls out "Crows" or "Cranes", the team called must turn around and try to outrun opponents to marked safety line, without being tagged.

STRANGE CENTIPEDE
  Sitting on the ground, one behind the other, a group of players hook their legs around the waist of the person in front. Then, players use only hands and "rumps" to try to propel the centipede forward.

ALL TIED IN KNOTS

While holding hands to make a circle, players step over, under, and around arms, legs, and bodies to form a "human knot". Then, a chosen "foreman" instructs the group on how to untangle the knot.

GAMUT OF GAMES

Play some fun games like Tug-o'-War, Dodge Ball, British Bulldog, Leapfrog, Prisoner's Base, Flying Dutchman, Red Rover, or have Crab, Wheelbarrow, or Three-Legged Races.

SITTING GAMES

JOLLY JACKS

Scatter sixteen jacks on pavement. Then, all with one hand, bounce ball, pick up one jack without touching any others, and catch ball before it bounces again. On the next bounce, pick up two jacks, then three, and so on.

CLAPPING CLUB

With a partner, follow clapping sequences to favorite clapping verses, such as "Concentration", "A Sailor Went to Sea, Sea, Sea", "Did You Ever, Ever, Ever?", "See See my Playmate", "Who Stole the Cookies?", etc.

MYSTERY LEADER

Players sit in a circle and follow the changing actions of a chosen leader (Ie. Clapping, snapping fingers, etc.) Meanwhile, the chosen "inspector" must watch carefully to determine who the Mystery Leader is, who then becomes the new inspector.

TRICKS AND GAMES

Borrow a book from the library to learn some neat string games, such as "Cat's Cradle", or some fancy Yo-Yo tricks.

TASTY TREATS

HEALTHY CLASS PARTY TREATS

FRUIT OR VEGGIE KABOBS
On toothpicks, skewer pieces of fruit (ie. apple, orange, banana, melon balls, seedless grapes, etc) or veggies (ie. cherry tomatoes, cucumber, cauliflower, etc.) Dip fruit in lemon water to prevent darkening.

HAM & CHEESE STIX

Roll a small piece of ham or salami around a chunk of cheese. Secure by piercing with a toothpick.

CRACKER "JACKS"

round cracker
cheese slice
ham or salami
green olive sl.
mushroom sl.
half pickle

cracker
p. butter
banana
peanut
raisins

CELERY BOATS
Stuff pieces of celery with Cheese Whiz, cream cheese, or peanut butter. Sprinkle on sunfl. or sesame seeds. Insert a cucumber wedge for a sail.

G O R P

Mix together 1 cup each of any of the following:

- peanuts
- pumpkin/sunflower seeds
- raisins
- dried fruit
- carob or chocolate chips
- pretzels

NOTE: ALSO SEE RECIPES FOR COLORED HOLIDAY POPCORN, SUGARLESS FINGER JELLY, HEALTHY YOGHURT POPS, FONDUE RECIPES, ETC.

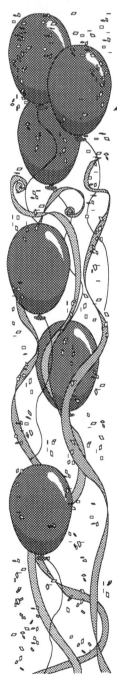

COLORED HOLIDAY POPCORN

INGREDIENTS

2/3 C. butter or margarine
1 1/2 C. white sugar
1 C. corn syrup
2 packages Kool-Aid
  (Ie. Red for Valentine's Day,
     orange for Hallowe'en, etc.)
1 tsp. baking soda
16 C. popcorn (1/2 C. kernels)

METHOD

Mix first four ingredients together and heat to boiling point, stirring frequently. Boil for 2 minutes. Remove from heat and stir in baking soda until foamy. Quickly mix in popcorn. To prevent globbing, spread popcorn out on pan to cool.

Variation: In a pinch, use one package Jell-o powder instead of Kool-Aid, and reduce sugar to 1/4 C.

CARAMEL CORN

INGREDIENTS

1 C. butter or margarine
1 C. brown sugar
1/2 C. corn syrup
1 tsp. cream of tartar
1/2 tsp. baking soda
10 - 12 C. popcorn (3/8 C. kernels)
1 C. peanuts, unblanched almonds,
    or pecan halves

METHOD

Boil together first four ingredients.
Remove from heat and add baking soda.
Stir until foamy. Mix in popcorn and nuts.
For crunchy, non-sticky popcorn, spread
out on pan and refrigerate, or bake at 225°
for 45 minutes.

SUGARLESS FINGER JELLY

INGREDIENTS

1 can unsweetened apple
   juice concentrate, thawed
3 - 7 g packages unflavored gelatin
1 2/3 C. boiling water

METHOD

Dissolve gelatin in boiling water.
Stir in juice concentrate. Pour into oiled
9" x 13" cake pan, and chill in fridge for
three hours or so. When firm, cut into
squares or make shapes with cookie
cutters.

Note: Finger Jelly may be redissolved
       (boiled) and set again, if necessary.

YUMMY YOGHURT POPS

REGULAR VERSION

Mix together 2 C. flavoured yoghurt and 1 C. milk. Pour into Popsicle moulds, or ice cube trays with a Popsicle stick inserted into each cube when partially frozen. Freeze until firm.

SUGARLESS VERSION

In a blender, blend together 1 C. plain yoghurt, 1/2 C. unsweetened pineapple or orange juice, and 1- 2 C. peaches, blueberries, strawberries, bananas, or whatever is available. Pour into Popsicle moulds and freeze.

For those hot, sunny days!

FUDGESICLES

INGREDIENTS

2 C. chocolate ice cream
2 C. chocolate milk
   (or 2 C. white milk mixed with
   3 Tbsp. hot chocolate powder)

METHOD

Working quickly, whisk together milk and ice cream. Pour into Popsicle moulds (or ice cube trays with Popsicle sticks inserted after partially frozen). Freeze until firm, and enjoy!

MILKSHAKE

INGREDIENTS

2 C. (6 - 8 scoops) ice cream
2 C. milk
1 tsp. vanilla
1 or 2 bananas, or 1/2 C. berries (opt.)

METHOD

Combine ingredients in a blender. With adult supervision, cover with lid and blend for about 20 seconds.

COOL CONE CAKES

INGREDIENTS

Cake mix (any flavor)
12 flat-bottomed cones
2 C. frosting
Decorations (ie. sprinkles,
   coconut, chocolate chips,
   ju jubes, Smarties , etc.)

METHOD

Prepare cake batter as per package.
Spoon 3 - 4 Tbsp. of batter into each
cone. On a cookie   sheet or cake pan,
bake at 350° F for 25 minutes. Cool.
Ice top of cones, and decorate.

HEALTHY
MONSTER COOKIES

INGREDIENTS
1 C. wholewheat flour
2 C. rolled oats
1/4 C. wheatgerm
1 tsp. baking soda
3/4 C. butter or margarine
1 C. brown sugar
2 eggs
1 tsp. vanilla
3/4 C. raisins, choc. chips, or Smarties
1/4 C. sesame seeds (opt.)

METHOD
In large bowl mix together first four ingredients. In small bowl, blend butter or margarine, brown sugar, eggs, and vanilla. Blend into oats mixture. Stir in last three ingredients. Press 1/2 C. of dough onto a cookie sheet to make a circle about 14 cm (5 - 6") across. Bake at 350°F for about 10 minutes. Makes about nine monster cookies.

Yummy!!

NOODLE CLUSTERS

INGREDIENTS

1 C. chocolate chips
1 C. butterscotch chips
2 C. chow mein noodles
1 C. salted peanuts

METHOD

Melt chocolate and butterscotch chips over low heat (or in microwave oven). Stir in dry noodles and peanuts. Drop in clusters onto cookie sheet. Cool. Makes about 2 dozen.

SUGAR COOKIES

INGREDIENTS

1 C. butter or margarine
1 C. sugar
2 eggs
1 tsp. vanilla
3 C. flour
2 tsp. baking powder
1/2 tsp. salt
Food coloring (opt.)

BUTTER ICING

Cream together
4 C. icing sugar
and 1/2 C. butter or
margarine. Beat in
3/8 C. milk and 2 tsp.
vanilla, adding more
icing sugar or milk if
necessary.

METHOD

Cream together butter and sugar. Beat in eggs, vanilla, and food coloring, if desired. Stir in flour, baking powder, and salt. Roll out dough to 1/8" thickness on lightly floured surface. Cut into shapes with cookie cutters. Bake at 350° F for about 8 - 10 minutes. Decorate with icing, and candies/sprinkles if you wish. Makes about forty mid-sized cookies.

STAINED GLASS COOKIES

INGREDIENTS

1 C. butter or marg.
1 C. brown sugar
2 eggs
3 1/4 C. flour (or less)
2 tsp. baking powder
2 - 3 pkg. colored Life-savers

METHOD

Cream butter and sugar. Stir in eggs. Add flour and baking powder and mix. Chill. Take small lumps of dough and roll them into 1/4" strips. Form these strips into diamonds, hearts, etc. on foil-lined cookie sheet. Crush up one color of Life-savers , and sprinkle into cookie outlines to cover bottom. Bake at 375° F for 8 - 10 minutes or until light brown. Cool, and peel off foil.

Note: 2 packages Life-savers fill seven 3" x 2" cookies.

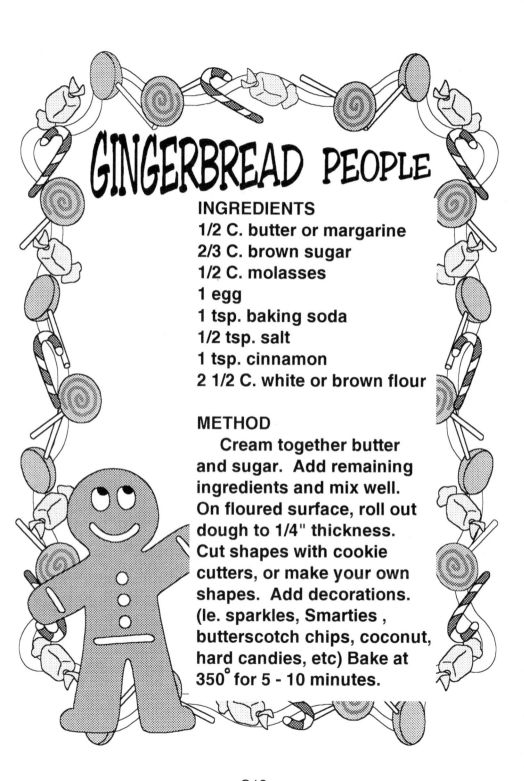

GINGERBREAD PEOPLE

INGREDIENTS
1/2 C. butter or margarine
2/3 C. brown sugar
1/2 C. molasses
1 egg
1 tsp. baking soda
1/2 tsp. salt
1 tsp. cinnamon
2 1/2 C. white or brown flour

METHOD
Cream together butter and sugar. Add remaining ingredients and mix well. On floured surface, roll out dough to 1/4" thickness. Cut shapes with cookie cutters, or make your own shapes. Add decorations. (Ie. sparkles, Smarties , butterscotch chips, coconut, hard candies, etc) Bake at 350° for 5 - 10 minutes.

NUTS & BOLTS

INGREDIENTS
1/4 C. melted butter or salad oil
2 tsp. Worcestershire Sauce
1/2 tsp. garlic salt
1/2 tsp celery salt
1/2 tsp. onion salt
2 C. Life, Crispix, or Shreddies
2 C. Cheerios
2 C. pretzels
2 C. salted peanuts

METHOD
Stir together first five ingredients. Pour over cereals and nuts measured into a large roaster. Mix well, using a spatula. Bake at 250° F for 1 hour, stirring every 30 minutes. Store in sealed container.

PIZZA BUNS

Give Mom a break!
Make your own lunch or snack!

INGREDIENTS
1 pkg. English Muffins (or hamburger buns)
1 can spaghetti sauce
Grated mozzarella cheese
Various toppings
(Ie. Ham, salami, mushrooms, pineapple, etc.)

METHOD
Slice muffins and place on cookie sheet. Spread on spaghetti sauce. Add toppings. Sprinkle cheese on top. Heat in microwave oven until bubbly (or broil in oven with help from an adult!)

TODAY'S SPECIAL

BEEF JERKY

INGREDIENTS

1 lb. lean steak, boneless
  (Ie. round, sirloin, or cross rib)
1/4 C. soya sauce
2 Tbsp. brown sugar
1 Tbsp. Worcestershire Sauce
1/2 tsp. ginger powder
1/2 tsp. salt

METHOD

Cut steak into thin strips (1/4" x 4"). In small, sealable container, mix together remaining ingredients. Add steak strips and stir well. Cover and refrigerate for 8 - 12 hours, stirring or flipping container every few hours. Preheat oven to very low temperature (about 145° F). Lay strips on a wire cooling rack set on a cookie sheet. Place in oven for about 9 hours.

DRIED APPLES

INGREDIENTS
4 - 5 firm apples

PROCEDURE
- peel and core apples

- cut into slices (rings) about 3/16" thick.

- lay slices out on cookie sheet and dry in
  145° F oven, with door open at least 2",
  for 6 hours or more.

- store in plastic bag.

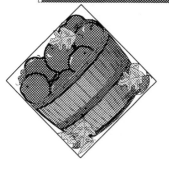

CHEESE FONDUE

INGREDIENTS
2 C. shredded Cheddar cheese
2 C. shredded Gruyère, Edam,
   or Emmenthal cheese
2 Tbsp. flour or cornstarch
1 1/4 C. apple juice or apple cider
1/4 tsp. garlic powder

METHOD
   In a small bowl, toss together cheese and flour. In a fondue pot or saucepan, heat apple juice or cider until it starts to boil. Reduce to simmer. Stir in cheese, a handful at a time, until melted and smooth. Add garlic salt and stir. Keep mixture hot, but below boiling point to prevent cheese from going stringy. Dip French bread cubes, bread sticks, apple wedges, and/or seedless grapes into mixture.

MEXICAN CHEESE FONDUE

INGREDIENTS
1 can cheddar cheese soup
1 can mushroom soup
3/4 C. mild chunky salsa
Large bag of taco chips

METHOD
   In a fondue pot or saucepan, mix together first three ingredients. Heat until starts to boil. Reduce to simmer. Dip taco chips into mixture.

CHOCOLATE FONDUE

INGREDIENTS
1 can Evaporated Milk (385 ml)
2 1/2 C. chocolate chips
Opt. - a few drops of peppermint flavoring,
or 3/4 C. peanut butter, or 2 tsp. of
instant coffee dissolved in a few
drops of water.

METHOD
In a fondue pot or saucepan, heat
milk and chocolate chips on low, stirring
constantly, until melted and smooth. Dip
any of the following items into mixture:
- - strawberries, orange sections, apple
slices, melon balls, kiwi or pineapple
chunks, grapes, banana slices,
maraschino cherries, and pieces of
doughnuts or pound/Angel Food cake.

BUTTERSCOTCH FONDUE

INGREDIENTS
1 1/4 C. whipping cream (1/2 pt.)
2/3 C. brown sugar
1 Tbsp. cornstarch
1/2 tsp. rum extract

METHOD
In a fondue pot or saucepan, mix together
first three ingredients and bring to foaming boil,
stirring constantly. Add rum flavoring, and dip
fruit or cake, as listed above, into mixture.

"TASTY TREATS" LIST

SENSATIONAL SLUSH
Fill a small yoghurt container 2/3 full with juice or pop. Cap with lid and place in freezer for 1 1/2 hours. Then, mix with fork every 1/2 hour or so until to desired consistency.

DRIPLESS POPSICLES
Dissolve one 85 g package of Jell-o powder in 1 C. boiling water. Stir in 1 1/4 C. juice. Pour into moulds and freeze.

FROSTY FRUIT
Wash, dry, and freeze berries, cherries, or seedless grapes in a sealed container. Enjoy on a hot day!

PRIZE PEANUT BUTTER
At top speed, blend together 1 1/2 Tbsp. oil, and 1 C. roasted, shelled peanuts, added gradually. When smooth, add salt, if desired. Store in sealed container in fridge.

BANANA ROCKET SHIP
On a paper plate, make an edible rocket ship, as shown.

- 1/4 banana
- pineapple slice
- cottage cheese
- star stickers

POPCORN MARSHMALLOW SQUARES
On low heat, melt together 1/2 C. butter or margarine and 64 large marshmallows. Add about 10 C. popped popcorn and mix well. Stir in a few handfuls of ju jubes for some added color.

CREATIVE CRÊPES
Follow a recipe to make simple crêpes. Then, fill with strawberries, blueberries, yoghurt, whipping cream, or whatever you have on hand. Pour sauce on top, if you wish.

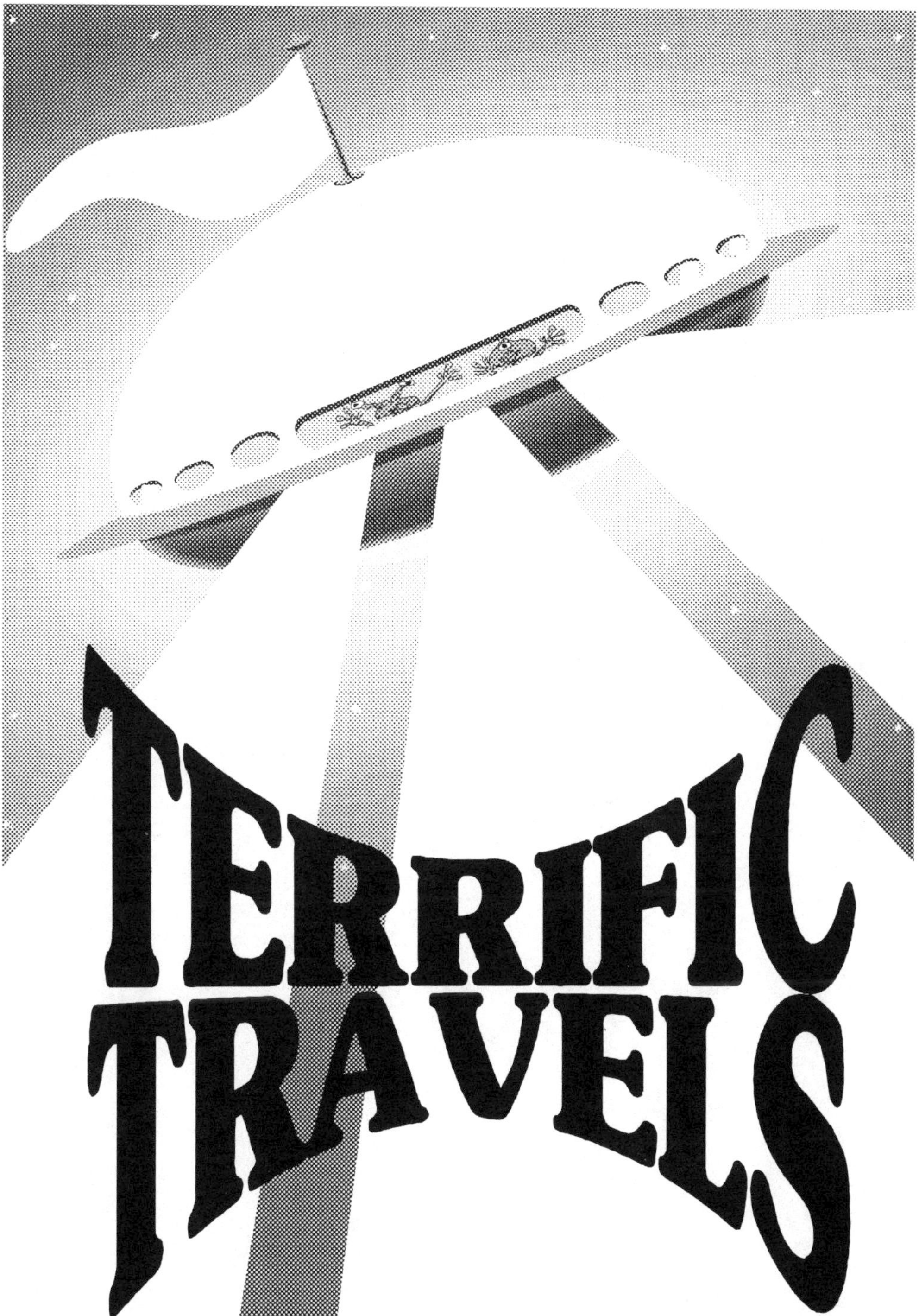
TERRIFIC
TRAVELS

Learn to speak "PIG-LATIN"

REALLY CONFUSE YOUR PARENTS!!
AMAZE YOUR FRIENDS!!

Think of a word, such as "bike". In your head, take the first letter of the word and move it to the end (Ie. ikeb). Add "ay" behind it (Ie. ikebay). Do this with every word you say, and carry on a secret conversation with your friends or travelling companions.

Note: Don't split up digraphs (Ie.- th, ch), or syllables that begin with a vowel. (Ie.- this = isthay, I'm = I'may)

CAN YOU DECIPHER THIS MESSAGE?

I'may oinggay wimmingsay isthay eekway.

Part. - *1 or more players*

Mat. - *pencil and Bingo charts below.*

Obj. - *to spot and tick off Bingo items to make a line or black-out.*

Proc. - *watch outside the car for the items listed on the Bingo squares. Lightly tick them off with a pencil as you see them.*

- *if you are playing with others, only the first person to see the object may print his/her initials in the corner of that box.*

- *the first player to make a line or black-out with his/her initialled boxes is the winner.*

Bridge	Tractor	Sidewalk	Dog	Red Barn
Horse	Gas Station	Police Car	church	Motel/Hotel
Exit Sign	Overpass	**FREE**	Stoplight	Yellow Car
Grain Elevator	Transport Truck	Greyhound Bus	Railroad Crossing	Speed Limit Sign
Garbage Bin	Motor Home	Minivan	White Fence	Machine Shed

River	Cow	Stop Sign	Restaurant	Airplane
Rest Stop	Bird	Blue House	Low Bush	Billboard
Moving Van	Truck Weigh Scale	**FREE**	Blinking Signal Lights	Oil Well
Mileage Sign	Barbed-Wire Fence	Wayside Telephone	Station Wagon	Pick-up Truck
Red Car	Litter	Motorbike	Train	Hay Bale

Little Tyke Version

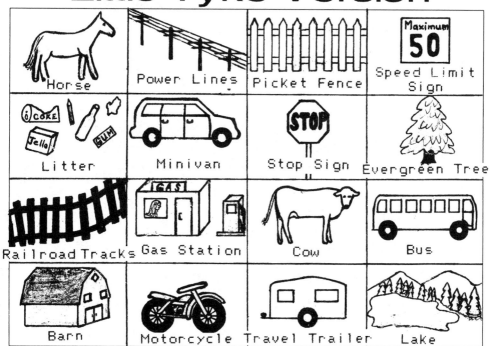

Horse	Power Lines	Picket Fence	Speed Limit Sign (Maximum 50)
Litter	Minivan	Stop Sign	Evergreen Tree
Railroad Tracks	Gas Station	Cow	Bus
Barn	Motorcycle	Travel Trailer	Lake

ABC SEARCH

Part. - 1 or more players

Mat. - none

Obj. - to earn the most points by being the first to spot outside objects in alphabetical order.

Proc.- players must look for an object, outside of the car, which begins with the letter "A", then "B", etc.

- only the first player to spot and call out the object gains a point.

- the game ends upon reaching the letter "X" (omit X, Y, and Z). The player with the most points wins the game.

Alternate: Instead of looking for objects, players must spot printed words on billboards, signs, etc. that begin with A, B, C . . .

STRIKE OUT!

Part. - at least 2 players

Mat. - none

Obj. - to continue adding a letter to a word being spelled without completing it.

Proc. - one player starts the game by secretly thinking of a word, and calling out its first letter.

- the next player must add a letter that will continue the word, and so on.

- anyone who is unable to think of a letter to add may challenge the previous player to see if he/she really did have a possible word in mind. If so, the challenger receives one "Strike". If not, the player who is unable to come up with an acceptable word receives a strike.

- any player who completes a word also earns a strike. After any strikes, a new letter is chosen.

- three strikes and a player is out!

HIDDEN WORDS

Part. - 1 or more players

Mat. - 1 pen/paper each
    - 1 dictionary (opt.)

```
HEMISPHERE

Sphere
Hem/s
Seep
Here
```

Obj. - to make the most little words from the challenge word within five minutes.

Proc.- players agree upon a challenge word found in a dictionary or in the list below, and record it at the top of their page.

    - within five minutes, players find and record as many hidden words as they can, at least three letters long, using only the letters found in the challenge word.

    - at the end of five minutes, the player with the most words wins that round. Check each other's lists for accuracy.

CHALLENGE WORD IDEAS - elephant, breathtaking, responsibility, ventriloquist, kindergarten, alphabet, disposition, intermediate, enthusiasm, instantaneous.

NEWSPAPER FUN

1. LETTERPRESS
"Glue" a letter to a relative or friend using only words or letters cut from the daily newspaper.

2. NEWSPAPER SCAVENGER HUNT
Tick off each item on the list as you find it in the newspaper. Can you find them all? Race with a friend.

a) a picture of a famous government leader
b) the price of the newspaper
c) a letter from someone
d) today's temperature
e) a number smaller than "one"
f) a picture of an animal
g) the horoscope of someone born on April 1
h) the word "sale"
i) a compound word
j) a picture of someone wearing a hat
k) a job opportunity for a nurse
l) the name of a place outside of North America
m) the city with the highest temperature
n) the name of a baby just born
o) a map
p) a news story from your capital city
q) a number greater than a million (1,000,000)
r) the score of a recent hockey or baseball game
s) the name of a restaurant

20 QUESTIONS

Part. - 3 or more players

Mat. - none

Obj. - to be the first to guess the mystery object in 20 or less Yes/No questions.

Proc.- player #1 thinks of a mystery object.

- in turn, remaining players ask up to a total of 20 Yes/No questions in effort to discover the mystery object. (Ie. - Is it an animal?)

- instead of asking a question, a player may use his/her turn to make one guess at the object. A successful guesser gets to choose the next mystery object.

- if the object is still undiscovered after 20 questions, player #1 reveals it and then takes another turn.

SILENT SEVENS

Part. - at least 2 players

Mat. - none

Obj. - to avoid elimination by replacing numbers with "7" in them, or multiples of 7, with the word "buzz".

Proc.- going at a fast pace, in a clockwise direction, players count off to 100.

- players replace any numbers with "7" in them. (Ie. - 7, 17, 27, etc.) and any multiples of 7 (Ie. - 7, 14, 21, etc.) with the word "buzz".

- anyone who forgets to replace with "buzz" is eliminated from the game (or after 3 strikes).

- the game ends when only one player, the winner, is left, or when players reach 100.

Variation - any number from 4 - 9 may be chosen as the silent number, or two silent numbers may be chosen.

MYSTERY NUMBER

Part. - 2 players

Mat. - 1 pen/paper

Obj. - to determine the mystery number in as few guesses as possible.

Proc.- one player secretly records any 4-digit number (le. - 8303).

- the second player records a wild guess at what the number might be. (le. 0372)

- the first player then evaluates the guess, giving a star * for any number that is correct and in the right place, and a dot ' for any number that is correct but in the wrong place. For instance, if the secret number is 8303, the guess "0372" would be evaluated as * '. (Always list the * first.)

- the guesser then uses the evaluation as a clue to make another guess, and so on.

- upon correctly guessing the secret number, players reverse roles, trying to beat each other's record.

BOXES

Part. - *2 or 3 players*

Mat. - *pen or pencil*
   - copy of dot paper found at end of book.

Obj. - *to complete the most boxes by connecting dots with a line.*

Proc.- *take turns drawing a line between any two dots.*

   - whenever you complete a box with your line, print your initial inside of the box and take another turn.

   - when all of the dots have been connected, the player with the most initialled boxes wins the game.

Part. - 2 or 3 players

Mat. - pen or pencil
      - copy of graph paper at the back of this book.

Obj. - to win the most points by completing the most "SOS' ".

Proc.- take turns printing an "S" or an "O" in a box.

      - if you add an "S" or an "O" to make a vertical, horizontal, or diagonal SOS, draw a line through it , give yourself a point, and take another turn.

      - when all of the boxes have been filled, the player with the most points is the winner.

ROCK, PAPER, SCISSORS

Part. - 2 or more players

Obj. - to be the first to earn ten points by winning ten hand symbol combinations.

Proc. - practice the following hand symbols:

"Rock"   "Paper"   "Scissors"
(fist)   (flat hand)   (2 open fingers)

- simultaneously, players make a fist and pump hands three times. On the third pump, each makes one of the three hand symbols.

- depending on the combination, one or more of you will be the winner. That is, Paper covers Rock, Rock dulls Scissors, and Scissors cuts Paper. For example, if you have Paper and your opponent has Rock, you win a point.

- the first player to earn ten points is the winner.

LONE MAIDEN

Part. - 3 or 4 players

Mat. - deck of number or picture cards,
        with about 18 pairs, and one odd
        card assigned as the "Lone Maiden".

Obj. - to collect the most pairs, while not
        becoming the "Lone Maiden".

Proc.- shuffle and deal all cards.

   - players lay down all pairs in their
     hand.

   - player on dealer's left starts by
     taking one card from person to the
     right. If a pair can be laid using
     that card, player takes another turn.

   - game continues until one player is
     out of cards, apart from the "Lone
     Maiden" card.

   - player with the most pairs wins,
     unless he/she is the "Lone Maiden".

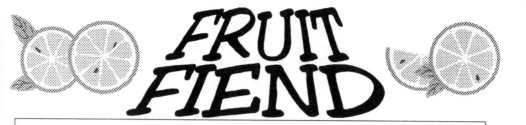

FRUIT FIEND

Part. - 2 - 6 players

Mat. - 1 copy each of "Fruit Fiend" grid on next page.
    - 1 pencil/pen each

Obj. - to be the last player to still have fruit left on the grid.

Proc.- record the name of each player beside "NAME____".

- secretly draw one grape cluster, two pears, three bananas, and four oranges on your grid. The squares containing identical fruits must be kept together in a horizontal, vertical, or diagonal line.

- player #1 makes the first guesses by calling out four blocks (ie. B7), on open squares (unless he/she is willing to forfeit fruit of his/her own). All players record a "1" in each square called, and then announce any fruit gobbled up (but not locations). Then, everyone records a "1" in the appropriate box below the names of the players hit. This will give clues as to the vicinity of other fruit belonging to those persons.

- players record a "2" in squares called in Round 2, and so on.

- a player may only fire shots equal to the number of fruit types which he/she still has left. (Ie. If all three bananas have been devoured, only three shots are allowed.)

- the game ends when only one player, the winner, is left with fruit still on the grid..

H15

FRUIT FIEND GRID

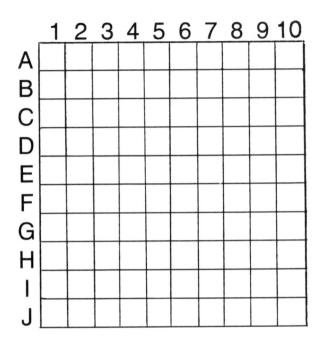

	1	2	3	4	5	6	7	8	9	10
A										
B										
C										
D										
E										
F										
G										
H										
I										
J										

Name _____   Name _____   Name _____

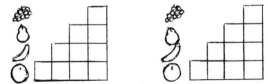

Name _____   Name _____   Name _____

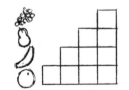

"TERRIFIC TRAVELS" LIST

INDEPENDENT ACTIVITIES

BUMP - ALONG PICTURES
    Without looking, hold your pencil on your page and let it move with the bumps and jolts of the car. Now, look at your page and color in pictures or designs that you find in your scribbles.

MAGNET MAZE
    Take along a magnet board with letter or picture magnets, or a magnetic board game (Ie. Scrabble) to play with on long trips.

TAPE TONIC
    Listen to your favorite song or story tapes to pass the time.

WORDSEARCH WHIM
    Use a copy of the graph paper at the back of this book to make a wordsearch. Record hidden words underneath.

PARTNER OR GROUP GAMES

TOWN TAILS
    In turn, players name a place (Ie. town, city, country, body of water, etc.) that begins with the last letter of the one named by the previous player. No place may be named twice. A miss results in elimination.

WORD WIZARD
    Within a time limit of two minutes, players record as many words as they can beginning with a selected letter. The longest list wins.

"TERRIFIC TRAVELS" LIST continued . . .

CAR COUNT
In turn, count the number of cars that pass by within your assigned minute. The player with the highest car count wins.

WHALE OF A TALE
Begin a story by relating an exciting first line. In turn, players continue the story by adding more sentences.

IN MY SUITCASE
In turn, players recite the phrase, "In my suitcase, I took _____", adding an item to the list each turn. Incorrect order or an omission results in elimination.

BACK-TALK
Use your finger to print secret messages on the back of a travelling companion. If his/her interpretation is correct, switch roles.

SERIOUS AS A JUDGE
Without touching the chosen "judge", make funny faces and/or sounds to make him/her smile or laugh. At this point, a new "judge" is chosen.

BLINK
Facing your opponent, see who can stare the longest without blinking.

FAMILY FUN
Share crazy jokes or stories, or sing favorite songs together. Well-known games such as I Spy, Gossip, Hangman, Tic Tac Toe, Pictionary, etc. are fun ways to pass the time too!

DOT PAPER

GRAPH PAPER

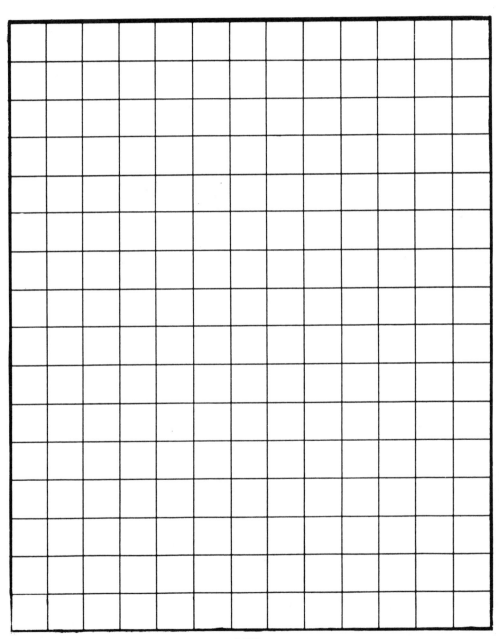

INDEX

BIBLIOGRAPHY

1   (Page A16 - Fun for Little 'Uns)
2 - 4 (Pages D16, D19, D20 - Partner Challenge)

Currah, Joanne, Felling, Jane, Box Cars & One-Eyed Jack,
(Box Cars & One-Eyed Jack Publishing Co., Edmonton, 1989).
(To order this book, phone (403) 440-MATH.)

GRAPHICS ACKNOWLEDGEMENTS

COMPUTER GRAPHICS - credited to Broderbund Software, Inc.
                    (Print Shop Deluxe, 1992)

PAGE 69 - Woodlot Discovery Kit, John Jantzen Nature Centre.

Hi, there!! To use

"HELP! I'M BORED!"

as a FUND RAISER for

your organization, write to the

address on the back of this page.

Shipping Address

Name _____

Address _____

City _____ Prov./State _____

Postal Code/Zip _____ Tel.(   ) _____

MAIL ORDER FORM

To order this book, please send cheque or money order, and
completed form below to:

Bluebell Cockle Shell Books
14020 - 123 Street
Edmonton, Alberta, T5X 4K3

* Please complete both sides of order form.
* After 1997, phone 456-9753 or 922-5284 to confirm address.

Please send me "Help! I'm Bored!" at:

$14.95 + $1.50 + $1.15 = $17.60 x _____ = _____
      (Postage) (GST for   (# of Bks)   (Total)
              Canadians)

* Prices subject to change.